Japanese Religion in the Modern Century

Japanese Religion
in the Modern Century

Shigeyoshi Murakami

Translated by

H. Byron Earhart

UNIVERSITY OF TOKYO PRESS

Publication assisted by a grant from the Ministry of Education, Science and Culture and The Japan Foundation

Translated from the Japanese original NIHON HYAKUNEN NO SHŪKYŌ (Kōdansha, 1968)

English translation © 1980 UNIVERSITY OF TOKYO PRESS
UTP Number 3014–16116–5149
ISBN 0–86008–260–1

Contents

Translator's Preface   vii
Translator's Introduction   ix
Preface   xv

 I Religion and the Meiji Restoration: The Bakumatsu
    Era to the 1890s
     1. Religion in Bakumatsu Japan   4
     2. The Persecution of Buddhism   19
     3. The Reintroduction of Christianity   33
     4. State Shintō and Sect Shintō   41
 II Difficulties in Modernization: 1900s–1910s
     5. The New Buddhism Movement   54
     6. Christianity, Forerunner of the Social Movement   59
     7. The Reorganization of Shrines   65
     8. The World Renewal Religions: Ōmoto-kyō and   70
        Hommichi
III Religious Oppression Under Militarism: 1920s–1945
     9. The Popularity of New Religions   82
    10. Persecution Under the Emperor System   95
    11. Shintō in the Imperial War   110
 IV The Age of Freedom of Religion: 1945–1970s
    12. The Separation of Religion and State   118
    13. New Religions in the Postwar Era   137
    14. The Political Advance of Sōka Gakkai   147
    15. Religion in Japan Today   157

Appendixes   168
Selected Bibliography   173
Index   179

Photographs follow page 79

Contents

Translator's Preface ... vii
Translator's Introduction ... ix
Preface ... xv

I. Religion and the Meiji Restoration: The Formation
    Era to the 1880s
    1. Religion in Bakumatsu, Japan ... 1
    2. The Perception of Buddhism ... 15
    3. The Reintroduction of Christianity ... 25
    4. State Shinto and Sect Shinto ... 31
II. Buddhism in Modernization, 1880s-1910s
    5. The New Buddhism Movement ... 37
    6. Christianity, Forerunner of the Social Movement ... 49
    7. The Reorganization of Sectism ... 63
    8. The World-Renewal Religions: Omoto-kyo and
       Hitonomichi ... 70
III. Religious Oppression Under Militarism, 1920s-1945
    9. The Popularity of New Religions ... 82
    10. Persecution Under the Emperor System ... 96
    11. Shinto in the Imperial War(?) ... 110
IV. The Age of Freedom of Religion, 1945-1970s
    12. The Separation of Religion and State ... 118
    13. New Religions in the Postwar Era ... 137
    14. The Political Advance of Soka Gakkai ... 147
    15. Religion in Japan Today ... 157

Appendixes ... 168
Selected Bibliography ... 171
Index ... 177

Photographs follow page 75.

Translator's Preface

The intention of this translation is to make available to Western readers the information and insights contained in Professor Murakami's Japanese book, *Nihon hyakunen no shūkyō*. The translation follows the original as closely as possible, but the following procedures in rendering the work into English are worth mentioning.

Japanese terms do not always translate directly into English, especially the titles of societies and religions. Where there is an accepted English translation, such as the Liberal Democratic Party (for Jiyūminshutō), such accepted translation has been used. Where a Japanese title has come to be well known, such as the name of the new religion Sōka Gakkai, the title has been left untranslated. For some lesser known societies, and for clarification, literal translation of some titles has been provided.

A book written for a Japanese audience naturally assumes greater knowledge of Japanese culture and history, such that a literal translation of some passages would leave Western readers in the dark. In those instances where historical facts would not be obvious to Western readers, some explanations have been inserted in the text. However, the translator's only insertions in the text are for the purpose of clarification, and there has been no modification of the author's argument.

Those readers more familiar with Japanese language and culture may wish to know some of the special Japanese terms that appear in the original. For this reason, a number of romanized Japanese terms have been indicated in the text (in parentheses) or explained in footnotes. For those who wish to pursue the subject further, a Selected Bibliography of English-language materials has been appended to the translation.

The author provided invaluable help in correcting several

versions of the translation, but of course any remaining errors are the responsibility of the translator. The translator gratefully acknowledges support which helped make this translation possible: an American Council of Learned Societies, and Social Science Research Council Joint Grant on East Asia for the summer of 1970, when the book was first read; a Western Michigan University Research Fellowship for the summer of 1977, when the translation was completed. Special thanks go to Mrs. Dolores Condic for typing several drafts of the manuscript. The assistance and patience of the University of Tokyo Press has been greatly appreciated, especially that of Nina Raj, editor, International Publications Department.

The translation is dedicated to the late Professor Hori Ichirō, who kindly encouraged and generously assisted me in my study of Japanese religion; it was Professor Hori who suggested that I undertake this translation.

Translator's Introduction

It is a pleasure to introduce Professor Murakami's book to Western readers, who stand to learn a great deal from it not only about Japanese religion but also about recent Japanese history in general. Professor Murakami has written extensively in Japanese on such subjects as folk religion and State Shintō, and especially on the new religions, but this is his first book-length work to be published in English. It is also the first work to appear in a Western language that explores systematically the relationship between modern religion and social, economic, and political conditions in Japan. His book has great significance both because of the nature of the subject matter, Japan's modern century, and for the insight that he has brought to bear upon it. It is difficult to overstate the significance of the century Professor Murakami has chosen to survey, which is known more for its political and economic events than its religious developments.

The roots of modern Japan extend back into the Tokugawa period (1600–1867) and beyond, but it is well known that it was the Meiji Restoration of 1868 that was instrumental in propelling Japan into the modern world as a nation-state. Generally speaking, "feudal" Japan emerged as a modern nation-state that saw remarkable changes in Japanese life. Japan had been primarily rural and agricultural, but this gave way to urban and industrial development as the previously developed urban and commercial centers expanded greatly. The feudal dictatorship was abandoned for a symbolic emperor and a kind of parliamentary government. Leaving behind two centuries of deliberate isolation prior to the Meiji Restoration, Japan entered international politics with a flash, being victorious both in the Sino-Japanese War of 1894–95 and the Russo-Japanese War of 1904–5.

Universal education was part of the general plan for mobilizing national industrial and military strength, and in the first half of the present century, Japan used this combined strength to become a major international power. And although not victorious in World War II, Japan emerged with an "economic miracle" of industrial recovery and international commercial success.

It is especially the industrial and commercial success of Japan that has attracted so much recent interest from the West. Westerners would like to know the clue to this "success story," and whether it can be adopted in the so-called developing nations, or even in Western countries. However, scholars who have studied the modern Japanese century see it not as an uninterrupted progress toward a preconceived goal, but more as a continuing struggle among competing forces and ideas. There are differing opinions about the reasons for the success, as well as to the degree of success.

However one assesses this modern century, it is apparent that religion, and religious values in the broadest sense, have played an important role in the unfolding of this crucial period of Japanese history. Shintō-inspired theories were partial inspiration for the move to restore the emperor and oust the feudal dictator. Even though the plan for making Shintō the core of the new government proved unfeasible, Shintō played an important role in government and education until 1945. Buddhism had been practically an extension of the government during the Tokugawa period but was unseated in favor of Shintō at the beginning of the Meiji era. Nevertheless, Buddhism had forged such a strong tie with Japanese nationalism that it even provided the motivation for ultra-rightists (and some sensational assassinations). Confucianism, in the form of Neo-Confucian teachings, had provided the major political rationale of the Tokugawa feudal government and was officially abandoned, but lived on in the educational system and helped support patriotic values. Christianity, officially banned during the early part of the Tokugawa period, was still prohibited at the beginning of the Meiji era, but foreign pressure was crucial in removing this ban. However, allowing Christianity to enter Japan did not imply freedom of religion or equality among religions. To preserve its favored status, Shintō was later declared nonreligious (with the exception of some Shintō sects), and Shintō, as national ethics, was the only religious tradition that could be taught in schools.

In short, religion has often been an agent of political and economic development. But it should also be noted that religion was equally affected by these developing forces. It was especially external political pressures that helped lift the ban on Christianity; and it was the internal political push to unify the country that supported the determination of Shintō as nonreligious and the recognition of some groups as Sect Shintō. On a broader level, the changing social scene, such as the shift of the population from countryside to city and from agriculture to industry, tended to weaken the traditional patterns of Buddhism and Shintō and to lend strength to the new religions. But religions were not completely free to organize, and until 1945 not only the new religions but also Buddhism and Shintō were subject to government control and often persecution.

The end of World War II marked a new era for religion in Japan. For the first time complete religious freedom became a reality, but this has raised other questions. State support of Shintō was removed, and no state support of any religion is allowed. And yet the symbolic character of the emperor is still not well defined, and the "national" or "private" character of rites involving the emperor and the national tradition (such as the two important Shintō shrines, Yasukuni Shrine and Ise Shrine) remain in question. Religions were completely free to organize, but in the immediate postwar years there was difficulty in defining exactly what a religion was, to rule out those who attempted to use the new freedom as a license for taxation evasion. Other changes drastically altered the religious situation: for example, the land reform took away an important source of revenue for some shrines and temples.

The changing fortunes of religion in this modern era are more significant and broader than just the relative strength of organized institutions. Religion and religious values were an integral part of the long drive to national unity and economic success. On the popular level of public schools, the religious values of Shintō and the ethical concepts of Neo-Confucianism were used to instill young students with a sense of national identity and personal motivation. Indeed, Emperor Meiji said as much in his famous

1890 Rescript on Education. In the present century religious values were used consciously for the ideological purpose of supporting nationalism and militarism. After World War II, of course, all forms of thought control and coercive participation in religion were abolished, but the result has been, in part, a religious and moral vacuum, in part, a rush to construct (and reconstruct) religious world views. It may be a truism to say that Japan is a nation seeking an identity, and yet this modern century, particularly the postwar decades, is best characterized in this fashion. And those in other countries will be able to learn much from reading Professor Murakami's account of this struggle for identity.

It is difficult to assess Professor Murakami's contribution in interpreting this modern century, for there is no Western-language book that systematically and critically analyzes any period of Japanese religion in its relationship to nonreligious factors. Generally in the Western world these two Japanese subjects— socioeconomic history and religious history—have usually not been seen in close relation, but have been treated separately. Western studies of institutional and economic history have not delved deeply into religious subjects, and religious history has not been seen in close relation to nonreligious factors. Early studies on Shintō did emphasize the intimate ties between Shintō, on the one hand, and social and governmental units, on the other hand; however, with the exception of a few scholars such as Holtom and Fridell, such ties were treated more as the enduring character of Japanese society, rather than as the basis for continuing studies of the interrelationships in recent history. Western studies of Japanese Buddhism have tended to view Buddhism more in terms of its historical connection with earlier Buddhism, and more as a philosophical and religious view of reality, than as a participant in the shaping of Japanese history. Even the writings of Japanese scholars that have appeared in Western languages were usually by adherents of a particular religious group, and their scholarly work in introducing that tradition was an indirect way of advocating that group's existential solution to the human condition. (Perhaps the best example is the abundance of works by Japanese scholars on Zen; their enthusiastic acceptance and imitation by Western writers seem to point up a widespread Western tendency to seek exotic existential answers not burdened with the ambiguities and tensions of history.)

It is not that Western scholars have denied the relationship between Japanese religion and Japanese history; rather, in paying lip service to this dictum, they have then tended to neglect the careful analysis of historical events that would reveal the exact nature of the relationship. All Western works dealing with the state and nationalism in Japan acknowledge the significance of religious or semireligious influence, just as most works on Japanese religion recognize the role of the state—both positively and negatively—in the history of religion. But there are few works which examine these subjects together. Some Western scholars have noted the role of traditional values in supporting national goals, such as Holtom for Shintō and Warren W. Smith for Confucianism, but they have not made a complete analysis of the entire social setting.[1] Perhaps the closest comparison is with Bellah's widely known work *Tokugawa Religion*, which follows Weber's notion of the role of the Protestant ethic in the development of capitalism, and explores the role of popular Japanese piety in the rapid political and economic development of modern Japan. In terms of comparison, both Murakami and Bellah are concerned with the impact of religious values in action, rather than their ideal, abstract formulation. However, there is also a sharp contrast in the two, since Bellah views political factors as primary, whereas Murakami is closer to Marx in his interpretation of economic factors determining religious developments.

Murakami's approach is to consistently view religion and religious developments in terms of prevailing economic, political, and social conditions. He asks how religion is affected by these conditions and the impact of religion upon these conditions. This viewpoint differs sharply from writers on Japanese religion who attempt to state the religious and philosophical world view, or internal message of a formal system. If Murakami is not advocating a religious message, what is he proposing? He insists upon an approach for studying Japanese religion critically, and he urges a

---

[1] A German work, not listed in the Selected Bibliography, is Ulrich Lins, *Die Ōmoto-Bewegung und der radikale Nationalismus in Japan* (Munchen: R. Oldenbourg Verlag, 1976).

principle of freedom of religion. His prescription for studying Japanese religion critically is based on a viewpoint of the involvement of religion in the concreteness of historical realities, and a necessity to deal with religion on that level. Murakami's viewpoint is not so unusual for Japan, since Marx has been one of the major theoretical sources for postwar Japanese historians.

The result of Murakami's work is an overview of the last century of Japanese religion written from one consistent viewpoint. He is openly critical of religion attempting to control the state, and he is equally critical of the state attempting to manipulate religion. It is to be expected that not all will agree with his approach and his weighting of economic factors. But he has documented the cases of religious control of the state, and state manipulation of religion, such that Western readers can reach their own conclusions. What is more important is that this is a story little known in Western literature. This is one side of Japanese religious history and one interpretation that few Western readers have had a chance to examine. This reading should be a challenge to those who are more familiar with the ideas and ideals of Japanese religion and less familiar with religion in action.

Although not advocating a religious answer, Murakami is not anticlerical or antireligious. Rather, as a strong proponent of religious freedom, he feels that the state is best able to serve the people when it is not hampered by the interference of one particular religious group, and that individuals can best find their respective existential solutions when not hindered or coerced by the state. The author regrets that for much of the century he is interpreting, religious freedom was minimal, but he sees the postwar period as a success in terms of the opening of freedom of religion and the existence of religion as a personal and individual choice. He is critical of attempts to revive traditional notions of nationalism and militarism in the postwar period, but is guardedly optimistic about the future of religious freedom. Professor Murakami's work is a welcome addition to Western publications on modern Japanese history and religion.

Preface

Japanese religion in the past century has experienced two major transformations: first, the formation of the system of State Shintō in the Meiji Restoration of 1868, and second, the realization of freedom of belief at the end of World War II in 1945. Today, in the midst of a public discussion concerning the direct relationship between the former Greater Japanese Empire and the present Japanese nation, it is necessary to examine once more the meaning of these religious transformations. At the foundation of the system of State Shintō, the religious expression of the emperor system, was Shrine Shintō, which voluntarily renounced its own religious function in order to reign over all religions in a new role as supervisor of national rituals. Subordinate to State Shintō were Sect Shintō, Buddhism, and Christianity, which, as officially recognized religions, were each provided their own protection and special privilege. Independent religious movements of the people were viewed as heretical by the authorities, and they met with severe repression and interference. As long as the government advocated its own religious character and determined the orthodoxy or heresy of a religion, it was inevitable that severe suppression of heretical religions would be carried out again and again.

Sect Shintō, Buddhism, and Christianity constituted one element within the framework of the emperor system of educating the nation, thus serving the state policy and cooperating in the war effort. Under a policy of unity of government and religion, the independent development of each religion was severely hindered. The government was vigorous in its control and utilization of religion; it never relaxed its vigilance over the possibility of religion developing independently and attracting the people. The separation between popular religious participation and daily life increased, and even within a religious state a general indifference toward religion developed. Thus, an extreme underevaluation concerning religion's social role became widespread.

With the end of the war, State Shintō collapsed, and the government declared its own non-religious character. In accordance with the actualization of religious freedom, each religion acquired the conditions necessary to recover its own functions, as found in a capitalistic society. Religion realized its social role. The established religions declined while the new religions—in direct contact with daily life and work, and offering religious salvation covering the whole of a person's life—occupied the mainstream of religious activity.

There has never been a situation in Japanese history in which one religion occupied a controlling position. In contrast to the racial and linguistic homogeneity of Japan, religions of diverse origins have coexisted, and down to the present a few of these religions occupy important positions as social influences. The state based on the modern emperor system reorganized Shrine Shintō, from the tradition of the ethnic religion of Shintō, and created a national religion. But Shrine Shintō lasted a mere 70 years. In Japanese society today, 230,000 religious bodies of various lineages (approximately 180,000 of these religious bodies are incorporated with the government as religious juridical persons) coexist. Without the premise of a strict separation of religion and government, there can be no guarantee of freedom of belief. The history of religion in Japan's modern century testifies clearly to this fact.

In contemporary Japan, religion is considered a private affair of the citizens, who possess both the right to believe in a religion and the right to be unaffiliated with religion. The Japanese people have experienced only 30-odd years of freedom of belief backed by the separation of state and religion. In order for this right to become a permanent part of the consciousness of the people, a long period of interaction between progressive and reactionary forces will still be necessary.

Today the movement for the revival of State Shintō, which is attempting to restore the religious character of the government, constitutes one branch of reactionary politics and is a challenge to freedom of belief. Another challenge to freedom of belief, in a different form, is the movement for the unity of government and religion which requires the direct linking of government and a specific religion to realize by political means a religiously conceived ideal world. This scheme presents a problem which should be criticized on its own grounds, clearly distinguished from the question of approval or disapproval of the political nature of the movement. The various arguments which are raised around this issue of unity of government and religion show that contemporary religious problems cannot be neglected. Believing in a religion, of course, is an individual, private matter. But the tendency of religious bodies to form a social force can exert both direct and indirect influences upon society as a whole. This is the reason for the necessity to be concerned with what religion ought to be, thus going beyond the consideration of religious belief itself.

This book surveys objectively the course of religion in the 110 years since the Meiji Restoration from the standpoint of freedom of belief. The 70 years of State Shintō, which was assembled out of the confrontation of the *kami* of the government with the *kami* of the people, constitute the history of the struggle to preserve freedom of belief. I only hope that this book might be widely read and serve as a guide for the study of the religious problems which Japan is facing at present.

I would like to express my heartfelt gratitude to Prof. H. Byron Earhart for translating this book and for providing an introduction and footnotes for this edition.

Japanese Religion in the Modern Century

I. Religion and the Meiji Restoration

The Bakumatsu Era to the 1890s

1. Religion in Bakumatsu Japan

Japan in the early nineteenth century was a mature feudal society. A feudal society is generally characterized by an economy based on agriculture, with land as its basic means of production. The feudal authority possesses the land, thus insuring the payment of tribute and binding the people of a feudal territory to the land. Several social features appeared in Japan, all of them conforming to the structure of the feudal society: a strictly divided class system, headed by warriors and followed by the three classes of farmers, artisans, and merchants; also, a value system taking the group as its standard, and a patriarchal system of ethics viewing man as superior, woman as inferior.

Agriculture, forming the fundamental industry, was regarded as the foundation of feudal control, and so the farmers were dispossessed of their wealth systematically and thoroughly, but since handicrafts and commerce were valued of secondary importance, merchants and artisans were less subject to such exploitation. The society of the *bakuhan* system involved a military government (*bakufu*) ruling over various feudal domains (*han*); this system is often called a late feudal society. The Tokugawa *bakufu*, 1600–1867 (which itself had the status of a feudal lord, and its possessions under the direct rule of the *shōgun*, or military ruler, forming the largest feudal territory), controlled the many semi-independent domains through a centralized authority. Throughout the eighteenth century under the *bakuhan* system, stimulated by the development of the power of agricultural production, there came to flourish both handicraft production centering on the manufacture of goods from farm produce, and networks for the sale of such manufactured goods which transcended the framework of the domain territories. The economic system centering on the pay-

4

ment of tribute in kind, which had formed the foundation of the original feudal society, was demolished from within; the rapid growth of commercial capital in the cities was so great that it threatened the feudal authority. The development of handicrafts in every region fostered an unorganized factory system of handicrafts and attracted a segment of the farm people as wage laborers. Japanese society of the early nineteenth century was a feudal society which already had entered the period of dissolution: the contradictions inherent in the feudal society advanced without ceasing, and in the sense that the *bakuhan* system of control intensified its own instability, it was a mature feudal society. The frequent occurrence of large-scale peasant uprisings and riots in the cities further endangered the position of the feudal leaders and brought the impending crisis to the fore.

Traditional Religions
Within a Weakening Feudal Structure

The contradictions in feudal society reflected sharply also in the world of religion. Most feudal governments are known to have their positions justified through religion. Even within *bakuhan* society, Buddhism, Shintō, and Confucianism had become vital supports of the government.

At the base of the *bakuhan* system, every Buddhist sect was an actual state religion. In the seventeenth century, in order to enforce the prohibition of Christianity,[1] a system was established under which each citizen's affiliation to a Buddhist sect was examined and certificates of membership to specific temples were issued. According to this system, the entire population was required to belong to a Buddhist temple, and the temples served the function of the smallest unit of feudal control. The *bakuhan* authorities considered Buddhism as an effective tool for controlling the people, and it guaranteed temple lands to the temples of each sect, thus supporting a feudal hierarchical order between main (*honzan*) and branch (*matsuji*) temples. By systematizing the relationship between temples and parishioners, it bound all the

---

[1] Roman Catholicism was introduced to Japan in 1549 by St. Francis Xavier and existed openly for about a century. Christians of this era and their descendants are called Kirishitan.

people without exception to some temple affiliation. The Buddhist priests, whose official status was assured, were in the position of the ruling class, and they administered education to the people according to the requirements of the feudal authorities.

Shrine Shintō, which in its beginnings originated from the indigenous ethnic religion of Japan, formed its doctrine and developed under the overwhelming influence of Buddhism, but it was placed in the status of a pure state religion which preserved the character of an ethnic religion and, at the same time, was subordinate to Buddhism. In the sphere of doctrine there arose anew several Shintō schools, such as the Yoshikawa, Watarai, and Suika, all of which drew elements of Confucianism into their doctrines. However, most Shintō shrines were placed under the control of hereditary shrine authorities, such as the Shirakawa school (which headed the Department of Shintō) and the Yoshida school (a dominant force in medieval Shintō). Shrine lands were guaranteed, and Shintō priests conducted rituals of Shintō-Buddhist admixture. In the powerful Shintō shrines the actual authority was held by such officials as *bettō* and *shasō*[2] located in dual Shintō and Buddhist establishments called *bettō-ji* (*bettō* temple).

The gradual disintegration of the *bakuhan* system of control was accompanied by growing public criticism and rejection of Buddhism and its close ties with the *bakuhan* system. Buddhism was, for the *bakufu*, an indispensable link of feudal control, but coinciding with increasing financial and political difficulties which the central government and many domains were experiencing, Buddhism's existence became a large burden. In the mid-eighteenth century are recorded the expansive figures which set the number of Buddhist temples in the entire country in excess of 310,000, with Buddhist priests and nuns totalling more than 415,000. Under the reforms of the Kyōhō era (1716–36), Buddhism had ceased to receive the preferential treatment it had so far received; the same tendency was also seen in the domains, which in an effort to economize, reduced their favors to Buddhism. From among the Shintō priestly authorities and hereditary shrine families, too, there was opposition to the power of Shintō-Buddhist priests, and in some regions movements arose demanding the dissolution of Buddhist parish ties and permission for Shintō funeral cer-

---

[2] *Bettō* is a Buddhist term for temple superintendents. *Shasō* are Buddhist priests serving in Shintō shrines.

emonies.[3] At the end of the Tokugawa period, in such domains as Mito, Tsuwano, and Satsuma where movements for restoration of imperial rule and financial reorganization were strong, temples were reduced and the Shintō side gained power.

The theories for the rejection of Buddhism advocated by Confucianists and statesmen possessed a concrete foundation: the resistance of the masses toward Buddhism, a religion that was a vital link in the feudal control system. There were also Tokugawa theoreticians who wrote against Buddhism. Andō Shōeki advocated a thoroughgoing egalitarianism based on the pattern of an agricultural economy, making a theoretical attack on Shintō, Confucianism, and Buddhism. The scholar Tominaga Nakamoto, a former Osaka merchant, wrote *Shutsujō Kōgo* on Mahayana Buddhism, a critical analysis of Buddhist thought which provided a broad foundation for anti-Buddhist theories. Yamagata Bantō, also a merchant-scholar, while supporting the feudal system, strongly advocated atheism and rejected the worship of *kami* and buddhas. The traditional criticism that Buddhism simply concerns itself with salvation in the future life and is of no use in the present life became widespread in late Tokugawa.

In the diffusion of Shintō to the folk level, a great role was played by the development of Shingaku, a teaching which originated with the Tokugawa scholar Ishida Baigan and featured the viewpoint of the unity of Shintō, Confucianism, and Buddhism. Shingaku, which became an integral part of merchant culture, set forth a popular philosophy of life which affirmed feudal ethics and merchant behavior. It taught Shintō ethics in an easily understood form and created a new style of mass education. A Shingaku society was organized to cope with actual social problems, such as famine and relief, and its activities exerted influence on the propagation activity of various other religious groups.

Capable people within Shintō denominations contributed to the propagation and development of thought. In late Tokugawa, reflecting both the revival of national consciousness which accompanied the development of a domestic market, and the instigation for unification of the people, Shintō once more permeated the

---

[3] One of the central features of the Buddhist parish tie was the obligation to have Buddhist memorial services performed for the dead of every family. Historically, Shintō funeral ceremonies have been the rare exception.

ranks of the masses, and Shintō lectures became popular. In the Tempo era (1830–44), the Shintō priest Inoue Masakane (1790–1849) advocated the Tohokami theory of the Shirakawa tradition of Shintō. However, because he included material criticizing the feudal government in his teachings, he was banished to the island of Miyake and died there. Umetsuji Norikiyo (1798–1861) preached Uten Shintō, which advocated the equality of the four social classes, and was banished to the island of Hachijō and died there. Together with the popularization of Shintō theories there appeared one after another new Shintō theories which appealed to the life of the masses and partially reflected the needs of the masses; these new theories were suppressed by the *bakufu*. Also, Kotani Sanshi (1765–1841) appeared within the tradition of Fuji pilgrimage groups, the center of all such mountain pilgrimage groups; he changed its doctrine along Shintō lines and advocated the Fujidō sect oriented around practical morality. This too was banned by the *bakufu*.

The Restoration Shintō of Hirata Atsutane (1776–1843), which arose out of the school of Kokugaku (National Learning) appeared at a time when Shintō was gaining popular acceptance. Kokugaku originally developed as the study of the Japanese classics under the stimulus of Confucian classical studies. Criticizing foreign thought, such as Buddhism and Confucianism, this restoration movement favored Japan's indigenous thought and ethics; it rejected feudal ethics and contained an element in which people tended to be captivated by emotionalism. However, that restoration movement consistently defended the *bakuhan* system of control, and their "revere the emperor" argument was emphasized as a theory supporting the government. Hirata Atsutane, the son of a warrior of the Akita domain, went to Edo and took up Kokugaku. During his lifetime he did not have an opportunity to meet personally with Motoori Norinaga, the chief architect of Kokugaku, but saw him in a dream, and interpreting this as an indication that he was permitted to join the school, became Motoori's posthumous disciple. Hirata did not agree with the contemporary tendency for Kokugaku to be centered in literature; he expanded Kokugaku into the religious realm and created a new Shintō theory. Hirata in plain words severely attacked the established religions of Buddhism, Confucianism, and syncretistic

Shintō, and provided new interpretations for the *Kojiki* and *Nihon Shoki*, the earliest Japanese chronicles. In Restoration Shintō, it is held that the creator of the entire universe is Amenominakanushi, the chief ruling *kami*,[4] while Ōkuninushi rules over the realm of the dead. However, Hirata learned the notion of a unique creator *kami* (or God) from secretly imported Christian writings in Chinese translation. Also Hirata created original rites for funeral ceremonies and Shintō prayers (*norito*). The rites, prayers, and doctrine of contemporary Shintō depended heavily on Buddhism and Confucianism. Restoration Shintō arose within this context of the underdevelopment of Shintō's religious content. Standing in the long tradition of the study of Kokugaku's "sacred scriptures," and although incomplete in itself, he prepared the way for a distinctive religious tradition. In 1840 Hirata's books were censured by the *bakufu*, and he was exiled to Akita, where in the midst of despair he died a natural death. His followers petitioned for a Shintō funeral ceremony but because it was not granted, they conducted a Shintō-style funeral service and then buried him at the parish Buddhist temple in a Buddhist funeral.

There were more than 550 disciples of Hirata, most of whom were townspeople and lower class *samurai* (warriors). At the end of the Tokugawa period, the movement to overthrow the military government intensified, and at the point when the claims for expelling the foreigners and revering the emperor formed a broad alliance for the overthrow of the military government, a dramatic change took place. The restoration movement of Restoration Shintō and the arguments supporting reverence for the emperor, which initially supported the feudal control system, turned into a fanatical antiforeign movement that called for overthrow of the feudal government. From the Bunkyū era (1861–64), the adherents of the Hirata school of Kokugaku increased sharply; this group organized upper- and middle-class merchants and artisans, lower-class warriors, and in farm villages rich farmers, local capitalistic landlords, and Shintō priests. In Restoration Shintō, which

---

[4] *Kami* is the inclusive Japanese term for divinities, spirits, cosmic and natural forces, venerated ancestors, and even revered humans. Throughout the book, the term *kami*, which can be either singular or plural, is left untranslated.

Amenominakanushi and Ōkuninushi derive from ancient Japanese mythology and appear in the *Kojiki* and *Nihon Shoki* as part of the Shintō pantheon, whereas Hirata's notion of divinity is thought to be an adaptation of the Christian notion of God.

expanded to embrace 4,000 followers, Hirata Kanetane (1799–1880), the adopted son of Hirata Atsutane who lived in Edo, held authority as the main house of the movement. Feudal lords supported Kokugaku, as in the case of the Tsuwano domain of Iwami (Shimane Prefecture), and there were some domains that changed the official teaching of their domains from Confucianism to Kokugaku. At the end of the Tokugawa period, the majority of the persons who joined the Hirata school were not the lowest segment of farmers, merchants, or artisans, who persistently sought out world renewal through uprisings and riots; rather, they were the upper-class warriors, who sought feudal and absolutistic reunification through political means by overthrow of the *bakufu* and restoration of imperial rule. For these people, the ideology of Restoration Shintō provided theoretical support for the political activity of the Mito school.[5] Restoration Shintō did create a novel systematized body of doctrine, but before offering up the substance of religion, such as rituals and ecclesiastical organization, it brought about its self-development as an anti-status quo ideology within the political movement to overthrow the *bakufu*.

New Religions of Living Kami

In its absolute control of the country, the *bakuhan* authorities crushed the power of established religions and forced them to submit to feudal authority. It suppressed Christianity and froze Shrine Shintō and every Buddhist sect in its contemporary status, and while supporting the established religious order, the authorities made every religion render service in dignifying and lending prestige to the feudal control system. The government and various domains consistently prohibited new religious movements or the formation of new sects that threatened the religious order and criticized the feudal system. There was a ban on new doctrines and heretical sects, and every religious movement was exposed to the danger of unceasing political suppression. In Tokugawa society, where belief in this-worldly benefits flourished, and the decadence and corruption of commercialized, secularized

[5] The Mito school of the Tokugawa period eventually supported the political movement for "revering the emperor and expelling foreigners."

Buddhist and Shintō priests was common, the government prohibited the independent development of any religions.

However, in late Tokugawa when the contradictions of the
feudal society heightened and the power of the rulers served to
deepen the instability, the established religions which formed
a link in the feudal control system suddenly forfeited their power
of spiritual guidance for the masses. New religions which captured
the aspirations of the masses began to grow. Religions featuring
new *kami* of the masses confronted the feudal religions. These religions developed as independent religious movements of the relatively low class farmers, merchants, and artisans whom Restoration Shintō was unable to organize. Their foundation was both
in the various cults of this-worldly benefits, such as *myōjin* (powerful deities), *reijin* (spirits of the dead), and *ikigami* (living *kami*)
which developed throughout the Tokugawa period, and also in
the voluntary religious associations (*kō* or *kōsha*) of powerful
shrines and temples and sacred mountains, which served as independent religious organizers of farmers, merchants, and
artisans. *Reijin* involves the belief that a person who in his lifetime
suffered from a severe illness, in the afterlife becomes a *kami* and
is able to save people who have the same affliction; this belief
came to flourish from about the middle of the Tokugawa period.
Also, in response to the desire for personal, this-worldly benefits,
one by one there appeared popular religious leaders who became
possessed and called themselves living *kami*, demonstrating
transcendental miraculous powers.

It was customary for these living *kami* to serve as mediums,
calling forth *kami* through specific procedures and causing the
kami to possess their own bodies, transmitting the words of the
kami to the people. In the religious consciousness of the people at
that time, possession by *kami* and certain animals was not considered very miraculous. Those who underwent possession were
believed to have extraordinary abilities: obtaining power
inaccessible to ordinary men, healing sickness, and granting
this-worldly benefits.

At the end of the Tokugawa period there appeared from among
these living *kami* founders who set forth new systems of doctrine
and promised salvation to the masses. The new beliefs overrode
the oppression by the *bakufu* and various domains, and put down

roots in the more developed farm villages of the Osaka-Kyoto area and western Honshū. From the middle of the Tokugawa period, religious associations of mountain pilgrimage groups and powerful temples and shrines spread among both farm villages and cities, and the practice of pilgrimages flourished. Thus the new religions established mass organizations centered around the founders.

Most of the religions born in late Tokugawa started from the belief in the living *kami* who provided healing of sickness and personal this-wordly benefits. These new religions—reflecting the mood of the times when feudal controls came to a standstill, and when the masses intensely longed for the arrival of a new age in the form of a world renewal through the power of *kami*—told of one great *kami* who would save all mankind and taught that through the power of this *kami* the salvation of the entire world would be brought about.

In terms of doctrine the new religions of late Tokugawa absorbed and inherited the various beliefs of earlier Buddhism, syncretistic Shintō, Shingaku, and folk beliefs, but in the content of their teachings there clearly appeared a new character not found in the religions of feudal society. The forerunner of these religions was Nyorai-kyō, founded in 1802 by a woman (later known as Ryūzen Nyorai),[6] a farmer of Atsuta (presently Nagoya). In this instance there was set forth belief in one savior *kami* quite similar to Christianity. Typical examples of late Tokugawa mass religions are such religions as Kurozumi-kyō, Tenri-kyō, and Konkō-kyō, and such lay Buddhist movements as Hommon Butsuryūkō, developed in Kyoto by the Hokke sect[7] priest Nagamatsu Nissen (1817–90).

Kurozumi-kyō

Kurozumi-kyō was founded in 1814 by Kurozumi Munetada (1780–1850), a low-ranking Shintō priest of Imamura Shrine in the suburbs of Okayama. Kurozumi suffered from a severe case of pulmonary tuberculosis, but in his thirty-fifth year while venerating the rising sun at the winter solstice he experienced the unity

---

[6] Nyorai is an epithet of the Buddha applied to various Buddhist divinities; Ryūzen is the religious name given the woman.

[7] Hokke sect, literally Lotus sect, one of the Nichiren group, which emphasizes faith in the Lotus Sutra.

of the sun *kami* (Taiyō-shin) and the Sun Goddess (Amaterasu Ōmikami).[8] Kurozumi came to believe that he himself was a living *kami* identical with the Sun Goddess, and, breathing in the sun's spirit,[9] he cured his affliction; then he preached faith in the Sun Goddess by means of magic and exorcism. The doctrine of Kurozumi-kyō held that Amaterasu Ōmikami created the universe and was the *kami* who nurtured all things, that all human beings are spiritual emanations of this *kami*, and as people practice austerities and entrust everything to this *kami* they are able to become one with the *kami*, such that their health is preserved and their businesses prosper.

The teachings of the ascetic Kurozumi spread among the warriors of the Okayama domain and also extended to the landlords, merchants, and artisans of western Honshū. At the time of the intensification of political strife in late Tokugawa, Kurozumi's disciple Akagi Tadaharu (1816–65) proceeded to Kyoto and in 1862 established the Munetada Shrine on the hill of Kagura in Kyoto. The shrine was designated as a site for imperial prayers, and, starting with a woman attendant of Emperor Kōmei, the number of believers increased among the nobility. Soon the shrine became one base of the "revere the emperor" movement.

The doctrine of Kurozumi-kyō is one of the Shintō theories that appeared one after another in late Tokugawa, but it gave all-out support to the feudal control system, and, by presenting a new outlook on life, offered peace of mind and this-wordly benefits within the system. By the Bakumatsu era of late Tokugawa, Kurozumi-kyō already had expanded with believers totalling 200,000, but it did not directly reflect the suffering of the people during this period of dissolution of feudal society.

Tenri-kyō

Tenri-kyō was founded by Nakayama Miki (1798–1887) in 1838. Nakayama was the wife of a landlord who was also engaged in

---

[8] In Shintō mythology Amaterasu Ōmikami as the Sun Goddess is the divine ancestor of the imperial line; sometimes, especially in Japanese folk belief, the sun itself is seen generally as a *kami*. The realization that the two divinities are in fact one constituted a deep religious experience for Kurozumi Munetada.

[9] *Yōki*, literally the sun's spirit, commonly means season, weather, or liveliness. The term appears in several new religions as the human vitality and joy resulting from religious harmony with the cosmos.

trade in a farm village of the Yamato plain (Nara Prefecture). She first experienced an intense possession when a mountain ascetic[10] was called to perform exorcism on a sick family member. Nakayama was possessed continuously for three days and nights, and in this condition stated that she herself was the ruler of heaven, descended from heaven in order to save the three thousand worlds.[11] Her husband Nakayama Zembei was very surprised and afraid of the power of the *kami* and replied that he offered up his wife to the *kami*. Nakayama Miki, through her possession, spiritually released herself from the pressures of the family system and its basically feudalistic, cumbersome restrictions.

Thereafter, through the Bunkyū (1861–64) and Genji eras (1864–65) Nakayama gained a reputation among the farmers of the area as a *kami* for safe deliveries and healing the sick. Nakayama was originally a devotee of the Jōdō (Pure Land) sect, but in the process of her intermittent possession she created a doctrine of salvation centering on this world, a change from the Buddhist emphasis on salvation in a future world. Tenri-kyō was a monotheistic religion believing in an *oyagami*, a parent *kami*. In the beginning the *oyagami* was considered the Tenrin-Ō, who turned the wheel of the Dharma (in the Buddhist belief of divine kings), and ruled over the entire world. However, with Shintō influences, it became Tenri-Ō-no-Mikoto (literally, Heavenly Wisdom King Lord).

Nakayama's propagation activity repeatedly was suppressed from the mountain ascetic, the Buddhist, and Shintō sides; to oppose this suppression, in 1867 she was able to gain the official recognition by the Yoshida school of Shintō of their *kami* as Tenri-Ō-Myōjin. At that time, Tenri-kyō was nothing more than small religious associations (*kōsha*) centered in the farm villages of Yamato plains, but after the Meiji Restoration it spread to the Kawachi plains and Osaka, and amidst the oppression of the new government gradually became a major influence. Tenri-kyō is a new religion which took root in the life of farmers. It created the hand gesture called *teburi* and the hymn *Mikagurauta*, based on indigenous traditions, cultivating a unity among the people with

---

[10] Mountain ascetic, *yamabushi*, a semi-Buddhist practitioner who engaged in periodic retreats on sacred mountains as part of his magico-religious program of prayers, rituals, and exorcism.

[11] Buddhist term meaning the entire world.

the same beliefs. Responding to the anxiety and suffering of the late Tokugawa farmers, it promised through Tenri-Ō-no-Mikoto the arrival of a "paradise of this world" full of joy.[12]

Tenri-Ō-no-Mikoto is a superior *kami* as well as a general term for ten *kami* in the Buddhist and Shintō traditions. The sacred land where this *kami* created mankind is considered to be the land of the Nakayama family in the village of Shōyashiki in Yamato, which is called *jiba* (center of the universe, symbolizing the place of creation) or *oyasato* (parent-village). When the destined time arrives, the *kami* takes the founder's body as its dwelling place and carries out the salvation of the entire world. This sacred tradition was gathered together in the sacred tradition called *Kōki* (or *Doroumi Kōki*) in the 1870s. Nakayama recommended the bright "joyous living" which followed from this faith. She taught that if one abandons the eight "dusts" (evil thoughts), such as parsimony, desire, envy, and greed, one realizes that one's own body is something borrowed from the *kami* and carries out earnest service to the *kami*, then a miraculous salvation will be granted.

In the doctrine of Tenri-kyō a humanism centered on people and this world, and the equality of man and woman is clearly taught; administrators are addressed by the epithet "high mountain" and the masses are called "valley bottom." A new quality absent in feudal religion, the insistent call for the material and spiritual relief of the masses, became Tenri-kyō's unique characteristic. At this time the hope of the masses was for world renewal[13] such that by the virtue of the *kami*, the world would instantly change and an ideal world would materialize. Typical of this hope for world renewal was the rash of spontaneous group pilgrimages (*o-kage mairi*) to Ise Shrine. Tenri-kyō was a religion that promised world renewal and generated group enthusiasm in religion.

Konkō-kyō

Konkō-kyō was founded in 1859 by a middle-class farmer Konkō Daijin (born Kawade Bunjirō, 1814–83) of Bitchū (Okayama Prefecture). Konkō was a firm believer in Konjin, a deity of folk

---

[12] Joy, *yōki*, is the basis for the crucial Tenri-kyō term *yōki-gurashi*, joyous living; the term *yōki* was also utilized by Kurozumi Munetada.

[13] World renewal, *yonaoshi*, a popular term for the hope for social renewal.

religion originally derived from religious Taoism,[14] but in this religion his influence was strong as the *kami* who imposed dreadful curses. However, on the occasion of his younger brother's possession, Konkō himself heard the words of Konjin, and realized through his individual experience as a single farmer, that Konjin actually was the ancestral *kami* of the earth, the supreme tutelary *kami* (*ujigami*) called Tenchi Kane-no-Kami.

Konkō taught the neighboring farmers belief in Tenchi Kane-no-Kami as a benevolent *kami* and not as a *kami* of curses, and he gained followers through healing and discussion of personal and agricultural problems. Konjin gave up agriculture and continually sat in the presence of the *kami* and mediated[15] the petitions of the believers; having prayed and understood the words of the *kami* he then transmitted them to the believers.

Konkō proclaimed himself a *kami*, Ikigami Konkō Daijin, (literally Living Kami Gold-Bright Great Kami). He held that human beings are all the parishioners of this *kami*, and when they give up desire, sincerely and respectfully believing, then *o-kage* (this-worldy benefits) would be received. Konkō-kyō criticized such superstitious folk beliefs as auspicious and inauspicious days and directions which darkly enveloped the life of farmers and taught that through belief the human principles of a bright, abundant life would be realized. Konkō taught the equality of all men as the children of the *kami*, and even if a warrior of high status appeared, Konkō treated him the same as he would a farmer. Late Tokugawa Konkō-kyō was directed toward an enlightened, civilized character with emphasis on the present world and human principles; this character contrasts with Tenri-kyō, which called for a religiopolitical revolution and realization of an ideal world. Konkō-kyō, which persistently has continued to seek out an inner salvation, may be called the germ of modern religion in Japan. Just before the overthrow of the *bakufu*, Konkō-kyō had extended its teaching to the farmers, merchants, and artisans of western Honshū; it became affiliated with the Shirakawa school of Shintō and founded the Konjinsha, or Konjin Shrine, at the

14 Religious Taoism is known in Japan as Ommyōdō, a loose collection of beliefs and practices especially concerning such matters as auspicious and inauspicious directions and days.

15 Mediate or transmit, *toritsugi*, the crucial rite of Konkō-kyō combining mystical communion and divine counselling.

Okayama headquarters. After the Meiji Restoration in 1868, the propagation of Konkō-kyō reached as far as the Osaka-Kyoto region, northern Kyūshū, the island of Shikoku, and Tokyo.

Hommon Butsuryūkō

Hommon Butsuryūkō, developed in Kyoto in 1857, is the forerunner of lay organizations centering their belief around the Lotus Sutra in modern times. Among the various sects of the Nichiren line which criticized the existing politics and society and favored a social ethic, in late Tokugawa there arose criticism of the rigidity of Buddhist sects and their powerlessness under the *bakuhan* system. As a result, movements of lay believers became active. This tendency was especially conspicuous among two sects of the Shōretsu branch emphasizing strict doctrinal interpretation: the followers of Nikkō, a major disciple of Nichiren, and the Hokke sect. The Shōretsu branch derives its name from its emphasis on faith in the "true gate" or *hommon* of the Lotus Sutra, the latter portion of that scripture.[16] Nagamatsu Nissen, the initial leader of Hommon Butsuryūkō, in his thirtieth year turned from the career of a merchant-scholar and became a priest of the Hokke sect. However, dissatisfied with the stagnation and corruption of sect affairs, and criticizing other Buddhist sects as man-made sects, he launched the Hommon Butsuryūkō of lay believers as a religious association (*kō*) founded by the Buddha for the spread of the "truth"[17] of Buddhism. Nissen left the priesthood and rejected the authority of temples and priests and preached a faith in the Lotus Sutra that was concentrated into one basic theme, that of this-worldly benefit. Nissen explained his teaching in simple poems, and his fellow believers gradually organized small groups of mutual help and study *kō*, fostering a strong group consciousness among followers. From late Tokugawa until early Meiji, Nissen repeatedly was the object of suppression and was imprisoned three times, but his propagation brought the merchants and artisans of the Kyoto-Osaka area into his main strength.

Both Tenri-kyō and Konkō-kyō confronted the established

---

16 The first half of the Lotus Sutra, called *shakumon*, is inferior, because the Buddha has not yet revealed his eternal nature; the *hommon*, the latter half, is superior, because in it the eternal nature of the Buddha is revealed.

17 "Truth," *shōbō*, a Buddhist term meaning the truth teaching; *shōbō* is equivalent to *saddharma* in Sanskrit, the first term in the title of the Lotus Sutra.

religious authorities, such as Buddhist priests and *yamabushi*, forming new religions in the midst of suppression by the authorities. The Hommon Butsuryūkō made a frontal attack on the sects forming a link in the feudal control system, organizing a movement of lay believers possessing their own livelihoods and occupations. The authority and order of the feudal religions were actually rejected, and amidst the decline of the authority of the *bakufu*, political strife greeted the terminal stage of the overthrow of the government. At the same time, the emperor's ancient religious authority was once more recognized and the political significance of the imperial court increased day by day. The imperial court revived shrine rituals, such as the annual Kyoto festival of Gion-e, and the rites in which the court, when confronted by external danger, prayed to large temples and famous shrines for national peace. Support for the emperor came especially from the "revere the emperor, overthrow the *bakufu*" forces, whose main power was the reform movement led by such southwestern domains as Satsuma and Chōshū. Together with the revival of Shintō, the authority of the emperor, too, was inspired with a new life, and rose up as the symbol of the reunification of Japan.

2. The Persecution of Buddhism

In the summer of 1867, just before the collapse of the Tokugawa *bakuju* and the beginning of the Meiji era (1868–1912), there occurred the *eeja-naika* disturbances. Since the previous year, the masses of the farm villages and cities had stood up against the crumbling *bakuhan* control system through the reckless world renewal riots and destruction stimulated by miraculous signs. Suddenly there fell from the sky paper amulets from Ise Shrine and other famous shrines and temples; people rejoiced as the paper amulets indicated the arrival of world renewal and groups joined together and began to dance. While they sang coarse songs irresponsibly ending in "Eeja-naika" ("Does it matter?"), they abandoned everything and danced in ecstasy, entering the homes of landlords and rich merchants, treating themselves to *sake* and food. These disorderly activities spread throughout the country, and everywhere the established order was thrown into confusion and paralysis. This was an explosion of the people's enormous energy, released when they fell short of their long-awaited goal of liberation from three hundred years of an oppressive system. The *eeja-naika* activities inherited the tradition of the *o-kage mairi* group pilgrimages to Ise Shrine which occurred periodically in the Tokugawa period; this activity developed into the belief of religio-political expectation whereby the world would change immediately through the sacred power of Amaterasu Ōmikami. In the background of this movement was the broad propagation of Shintō doctrines to the people. Liberation from the oppressive system was not expected to come through Buddhism, which had become a tool of the established system, but through Shintō, which penetrated and reflected the course of Japan's ethnic unification and

19

the formation of a national state. At this time, the religious authority of the emperor, an element inseparable from Shintō, became an ideological weapon in political strife.

Shintō and the Revival of Imperial Rule

The original fountainhead of imperial authority lies in the primitive religious function of the emperor as a magical king who is in charge of the fertility of rice for all the people in the Japanese islands, and who serves as the chief priest for the important rite of the harvest festival.[1] In order for the emperor to become the political authority for the newborn state featuring centralized authority, revival of the emperor's religious authority was indispensable; the revival of the policy of unity of ritual and government[2] established in the time of Emperor Jimmu,[3] was an urgent task for the new Meiji government in establishing its political authority. They did several things in order to "sell" the new political authority to the masses: they said that "concerning the honorable ranks of the venerable *kami*, though the highest rank[4] be present in various districts, it is because the Son of Heaven (the emperor) has granted these ranks that you are allowed to possess them; they said that the rank of the emperor was higher even than the highest rank, Inari-myōjin,[5] and they thrust to the front the religious authority of the emperor as the supreme head of Shintō.

In October, 1867, while the *eeja-naika* activities were continuing, the last Tokugawa *shōgun* transferred his power back to the emperor and the imperial court, thus announcing the end of the *bakufu* and its feudal control system. Immediately after the return of administration of the country to the emperor, the court

---

[1] Harvest festival, *shinjō-sai* or *niiname-matsuri*, is literally the "new tasting" when the harvest is offered up to the *kami*, and the emperor eats the "first fruits."

[2] Unity of ritual and government, *saisei-itchi*; this traditional phrase was revived as the slogan for the rationale of State Shintō and its unity with the political state. The general scholarly term is *seikyō itchi*, unity of government and religion.

[3] Emperor Jimmu, the legendary first emperor of Japan (as early as 660 B.C.), has always been a rallying point for patriotic and nationalistic concern.

[4] Highest rank, *shōichi-i*, reserved for *kami* and the highest deceased personages.

[5] The Inari shrines constitute one of the most widespread and popular of all Shintō shrine traditions.

made clear its conception of the new government, beginning with the revival of the Department of Shintō.

As soon as the revival of imperial rule took place, in 1868 the new government opened the Shintō Section in the Council of State, and once more revised it as the Shintō Office; then on April 5 it reinstituted the Department of Shintō and proclaimed its intention to return to the system of unity of ritual and government. The Department of Shintō was considered as the topmost government organ, higher than the Council of State, and in the revision of government in the following year, the system of two councils and eight ministries, in accordance with the ancient government organization, was realized. In the proclamation on April 6, the "oath ritual" of five written oaths was performed as the special Shintō rite of the emperor. This was a rite without precedent, in which the emperor set up a sacred *himorogi* tree in the southern palace and worshiped the heavenly and earthly *kami*. Gathering together all his officials, the emperor made an oath of the five articles of the new government to the various *kami*; next, court nobles and various marquises came forward in order and worshiped the *kami* and the emperor. On April 12, in the southern palace of the imperial court, on the occasion of the emperor's procession to Edo, the festival for war *kami* was held; beginning with Amaterasu Ōmikami, special imperial rites were performed for each of the various *kami* of war—Ōkuninushi, Take-mikazuchi, Futsunushi—praying for military victory. On June 29 in Higashiyama, Kyoto, was performed a national ritual for invoking the spirits of the nation's martyrs since 1853. On August 6, 1869, the Tokyo shrine to the war dead was established, where they enshrined only those imperial soldiers who died in the civil war of the Meiji Restoration. This shrine later became Yasukuni Shrine, the national shrine for war dead.

In accordance with the revival of imperial rule, the Shintō Office which the new government instituted had the functions of supervising the *kami*, rituals, Shintō priests, and shrine precincts. The proponents of Restoration Shintō were the main force in establishing the Shintō Office, as reflected by their prominent position in it, with representatives of the various Shintō schools, such as the Shirakawa and Yoshida, participating. This was the context in which they planned and executed the religious policy of the transformation of Shintō into a state religion. For example, Kamei Korekane (1824–85), an assistant supervisor concerning *kami*, was feudal lord of the Tsuwano domain, and was of the Kokugaku school. Leaders in the Hirata school of Kokugaku also were appointed within the new Shintō Office. These men were those who were originally behind the move to transform Shintō into a state religion.

The Separation of Shintō and Buddhism

Two days after the proclamation of the unity of ritual and government, on April 10, the government announced a directive, one provision of which preserved intact the *bakufu's* ban on Christianity. It stated: "The doctrine of the heretical religion of Christianity is strictly forbidden; if there be a questionable person, it must be reported to the authorities of the government office, and a reward will be given."

The government also ordered the return to lay life of *shasō* and *bettō*. The separation of Shintō and Buddhism was ordered by the councilors of the state, and they prohibited Buddhist words, such as *bosatsu* (Buddhist divinity), in Shintō shrines, Buddhist statues renamed as Shintō *kami* and treated as objects of worship, and the use of Buddhist ritual tools in Shintō services. Almost the entire country's shrines belonged to the various schools of syncretistic Shintō, such as the Yoshida and Shirakawa schools. Their rites and mystical practices were heavily influenced by Buddhist (especially esoteric Buddhist) magic and exorcism, and moreover it was usually the Shintō-Buddhist priests and *bettō* who ran the shrines. The reestablishment of Shintō's autonomy in accordance with the new government's religious policy of excluding Buddhist elements became an urgent issue. With the overthrow of Buddhism, Shintō burial rites by Shintō clergy were reinstated, a demand that Shintō revivalists failed to see effected during the latter half of the Tokugawa period. The power of the Shintō shrines was also restored. Former Shintō-Buddhist priests and *bettō* who returned to lay status began joining the Shintō clergy, and within half a year the government had to forbid this practice.

In November of 1868, the first year of the Meiji era, in the midst of the continuing civil war, the emperor proceeded to Edo (Tokyo), and Edo castle, which then became Tokyo castle, was made his imperial residence. He proceeded to the leading shrine of the Musashi District, Hikawa Shrine, and performed imperial rites there. He issued an imperial decree specifying this shrine as the tutelary deity for Musashi District. The following May, the emperor again proceeded to Tokyo and the transfer of the capital to Tokyo became official. But during his trip to Tokyo the emperor made an unprecedented pilgrimage to Ise Shrine. No emperor had made the pilgrimage to Ise Shrine since the pilgrimage of Emperor Jitō in the seventh century, and on the occasion of the pilgrimage to the Inner (Naikū) and Outer (Gekū) Shrines of Ise the special term "the emperor's audience" (shin'etsu) was adopted. The notion of the emperor as a "manifest kami" (arahito-gami) probably derived from the fact that he represented the apex of religious authority and the fact that he was of equal status with the great kami Amaterasu Ōmikami and Toyouke Ōmikami.

In August, 1869, the government's policy of nationalizing Shintō, centered in the Department of Shintō, assumed a positive posture toward "educating" the people through the establishment of apologists.[6] There was an incident in early Meiji in which some 4,000 Urakami Christians were arrested under the pretext of the ban on Christianity. The government excluded foreign "heretical sects," implanting in the people the ideology of the unity of ritual and government centered on worship of the emperor. In order to stabilize the foundation of the new government, they came to set up this special instrument of the apologists. The system of apologists became extended beyond its original conception, such that under the assistant supervisor for kami a host of offices were instituted: first the imperial appointee, the grand apologist; then officials whose appointment was approved by the emperor, vicegrand, middle, and vice-middle apologists; then the junior officials, the junior and vice-junior apologists; and the great, middle, and junior lecturers. Kokugaku and Confucian scholars were appointed to these positions.

In the following February, the imperial decree of a tutelary festi-

---

[6] Apologist, senkyōshi, literally the official who propagates teaching. Their "teaching," considered by the government as a way of enlightening or civilizing the people, was in fact a propagation of and apology for the new government.

val and the imperial decree of propagating the "Great Teaching" (*taikyō*) were issued. In order to propagate this great teaching through the apologists, on February 14 the emperor proceeded to the Department of Shintō and performed both special imperial rites and the opening ceremonies for the apologists. This Great Teaching was the doctrine of the national polity centered in the emperor, and the content taught was closer to national ethics than religion. However, the majority of the low-ranking Gpologists were former Confucianists and lacked an intensity in their propagation such that the actual effect of this "education" of the populace was rather far removed from the government's expectations.

Intensification of Persecution

In the meanwhile, the persecution of Buddhism (*haibutsu kishaku*) began throughout the country, and rumors spread about the government's attempt to abolish Buddhism. In May, 1868, just after the order for the separation of Shintō and Buddhism, there was a disturbance in the Hie Sannō-gongen Shrine in Sakamoto, at the foot of Mount Hiei. About 40 Shintō priests, along with scores of villagers from Sakamoto, broke into the shrine precincts with sticks and spears in hand. These Shintō priests, who had long been forcibly subordinate to the Shintō-Buddhist priests of Enryaku Temple and finally felt the time had come for them to revenge themselves of their long-standing resentment, demanded the keys to the shrine buildings from the Enryaku Temple priest, and his refusal resulted in a violent attack on a Buddhist institution. They threw out Buddhist statues revered as objects of worship and Buddhist scriptures, miniature Buddhist statues, and Buddhist tools. They trampled the objects, destroyed them with their sticks and spears, and finally started a fire and burned them up.

Large and small temples throughout the country were visited by similar anti-Buddhist storms instigated by the order to separate Shintō and Buddhism. These were temples that up to this point had received the support of the feudal government and domains and were now being trod under foot and destroyed. This spectacle of ruined temples was an event that clearly indicated in the eyes of the people the collapse of the feudal government and the restoration of the imperial court.

One example is the separation of Kōfuku Temple from Kasuga Shrine in Nara. The Buddhist priests all returned to lay status and became the "new Shintō officials" of Kasuga Shrine. Kōfuku Temple stood empty, and, in the interval, scriptures, Buddhist ritual implements, and furniture were carried away and sold. Many Buddhist statues were used as firewood, and the five-storied pagoda was auctioned off for a mere 250 yen. (A cabinet minister's monthly salary was about 500 yen during this period.) It is reported that the idea of the bidder was that because the cost of dismantling would be too great, he would burn it, but the value of the metals remaining after the fire would surpass 250 yen. Fortunately, the residents of the neighborhood feared spreading fire, so they opposed the idea, and the destruction by fire was stopped; thus the national treasure, the five-storied pagoda that casts a beautiful reflection in Sarusawa Pond of Nara Park, survives to this day.

The order for the separation of Shintō and Buddhism was an emergency measure for the purpose of making a clean sweep of Buddhist power out of the Shintō shrines. The government repeatedly explained that this order did not mean to attack and destroy Buddhism, proclaiming that "the instructions should be carried out peaceably." But the Buddhist persecution, led by local government officials and such people as the scholars of the Hirata school of Kokugaku, Shintō priests, and Confucianists, intensified in every district. In the Matsumoto domain, they abolished all Buddhist temples and forced the Buddhist priests to engage in agriculture. In the Toyama domain they left one temple for each Buddhist sect, reducing the number of temples through consolidation, and confiscating the buildings and ritual implements. In addition, abolishing temples through consolidation was carried out in other domains, such as in Sado and Satsuma. The Buddhist statues and ritual implements destroyed surpass enumeration.

What happened in this Buddhist persecution was that through the leadership of the lowest officials in the new government, the extreme anger of the masses toward Buddhism, as the basic link of authority in the hierarchy of the feudal control system, exploded. In areas where Buddhist persecution was severe, they destroyed the wayside stone statues of Jizō and Kannon,[7] and prohibited such age-old Buddhist customs as Bon (festival of the dead). In the regions where followers of the large Pure Land Honganji branch of Buddhism were numerous, such as Mikawa (Aichi Prefecture) and Echizen (Fukui Prefecture), farmers displeased with the political policy of the new government rebelled under the leadership of Buddhist priests and clashed with the officials of the domain. In the Mikawa area the farmer-devotees led by the young Honganji priest Tairei (1843–71) opposed the Buddhist persecution in Kikuma domain and raided the Ōhama government office, fighting against the domain officials until they were suppressed. This particular uprising was an attack of the masses against the severe control of farmers by the new government, an attack carried out under the banner of protecting Buddhism. However, excluding this incident which rallied for the protection of Buddhism, everywhere the Buddhist parties maintained a powerless silence in the face of the anger of the masses.

The decisive blow to Buddhism was the confiscation of temple estates. The new government, starting with the management of temple and shrine estates (which formed the feudal, material basis of the temples and shrines), restored to the emperor the registry of land and people. In addition, as a measure corresponding to this, on February 23, 1871, they confiscated temple and shrine estates and even brought under governmental control the administering and policing of such territory. Buddhist temples were thus deprived of their proprietary rights to possess land and their right to control the people. Among all the Buddhist sects, the confiscation order dealt its sharpest blow to the large Shingon sects, which relied heavily on their temple estates. But the Shin (Pure Land) sects, especially its Honganji branches, which relied mainly on its lay organization, were not greatly affected. In May, the system requiring families to be affiliated to Buddhist temples and to possess Buddhist certificates of affiliation was abolished, and Buddhist sects thereby completely lost their governing functions. However, in consideration of rights that temples and shrines had held heretofore, compensation in rice allowances and cash were continued.

[7] Jizō, patron saint of the dead, and Kannon, deity of mercy; except for Amida, probably the two most popular and revered Buddhist divinities in Japan.

The Rise and Fall of Restoration Shintō

As shrines also had their estates confiscated, they were in the same situation as Buddhist temples. But in the case of the shrines, their rank in the ancient feudal age was verified, and once more all the shrines were proclaimed to be the religion of the state. Already in June of 1868 a distinction between shrines for imperial rites (ranked major, middle, and lesser, comprising 29 shrines) and prefectural shrines was made. However, in July of 1871 seven levels of shrine ranks were put into practice, listed here from highest to lowest: 1) Ise Shrine (considered as one shrine complex, in a class by itself); 2) Kampeisha (imperial shrines), of major, middle, and lesser grades; 3) Kokuheisha (national shrines), of major, middle, and lesser grades; 4) Fukensha (prefectural shrines); 5) Gōsha (district shrines); 6) Sonsha (village shrines); 7) Muka-kusha (shrines with no rank). Also the hereditary system of shrine priests was abolished and a shrine staff organization with an appointment system was established. Shrine priests were guaranteed their livelihood and status as agents of the central and local government. Over 170,000 shrines throughout the country, each having experienced its own historically diverse career, greeted the Meiji Restoration. The small shrines with local ties—such as guardian shrines, tutelary shrines, and parish shrines—which constituted the majority of shrines served as the basis of farming and fishing villages' communal religious and festive services and were directly linked to the lives of the people. These shrines were of diverse religious origins, never uniform: shrines originating in nature worship and ancestor worship, private shrines where extended families worshiped, and shrines worshiping syncretistic Shintō-Buddhist deities for this-worldly benefits.

In order to support the nationalization of Shintō, the government made Ise Shrine the headquarters (*honsō*) of all shrines in the country, restructuring Ise Shrine as a centralized authority according to the doctrine of Restoration Shintō, and trying to make the shrines fill the political and educational role of the Buddhist temples under the *bakuhan* system. In local shrines originally there were many without a specifically named *kami* for worship, but these were arbitrarily assigned to specific Ise deities (*shimmei*) or *kami* revered in Restoration Shintō were imposed upon them. Furthermore, a regulation for a nationwide system of shrine parish affiliation was promulgated, again replacing the Tokugawa system of required affiliation to Buddhist temples. The government thus attempted to control the people by means of the shrines, which were to replace the now powerless temples, but this policy was unpopular, and two years later it was abolished when the modern census system was enacted.

After the abolition of feudal domains and establishment of prefectures in 1871, as the course of the new government became more stable, the policy of making Shintō the state religion was revised. The development of the enlightenment of the people from above, which took "culture and enlightenment" as its slogan, gradually altered the Restoration's initial Shintō revivalism, and a more realistic, effective policy became necessary. The leaders of Restoration Shintō either were defeated in their opposition to the establishment of another capital in Tokyo (in addition to the one in Kyoto) or participated in the riots of the movement to "expel the barbarians," and in the end they failed. In this period the Buddhist movement, beginning with Nishi Honganji, tried to regain its lost ground, and steadily achieved success, forcing the government to revise its policy toward religion. In the Nishi Honganji branch, from the end of the Tokugawa period the right of leadership of the local Buddhist groups returned to the Buddhist priests from Chōshū, who supported the revival of imperial rule. This fact insured their close connection with the leaders of the new government, many of whom were from Chōshū. Nishi Honganji led the way for other Buddhist sects by pushing for the absolute reform of the Jōdo Shin sect, and amidst the strong persecution of Buddhism they requested the establishment of the Office of Temples in the Ministry of Civil Affairs charged with the administration of temples. Having realized this, they were successful in halting the extreme persecution of Buddhism, and by 1871, it had ceased. The Tokugawa order of priority for temples first, shrines second was changed to shrines first, temples second, but the actual power of temples did not waver, and again the government was forced to recognize the relative position Buddhism occupied within its religious policies.

The Meiji government gradually began to turn away from the influence of the Restoration Shintō leaders. In September of 1871, the Department of Shintō was lowered in status to the Shintō Ministry, which was under the jurisdiction of the Council of State. The propagation of the Great Teaching by the apologists flourished, and in order to oppose the advance of Christianity the government withdrew its direct efforts to make Shintō a national religion. It adopted a policy of organized indoctrination using Shintō, Buddhism, and the various folk religious traditions. The Shintō Ministry was abolished the following year, and taking into account the demands of Buddhist organizations, the Ministry of Religious Education was founded. The emperor dedicated the three sacred regalia of the imperial throne (a mirror, sword, and jewel) and personally established a shrine for the performance of Shintō ceremonies. This supported the framework for the unity of ritual and government and at the same time a policy was enforced for the propagation of the emperor system and the administration of religion for political ends.

The Ministry of Religious Education acted as the agent of propagation for disseminating the Great Teaching while sacred rites and celebrations came under the jurisdiction of the Rites Office of the Council of State. As the emphasis of religious policy shifted to a unified, organized national education based on a Shintō nationalism, moral instructors (kyōdōshoku) were appointed in place of the apologists in the Ministry of Religious Education. This educational guidance and thought control promoting the ideology of the unity of religion and state implanted emperor worship among the people and aimed at the establishing of popular spiritual support for the imperial government. The month after the establishment of the Ministry of Religious Education, the "Three Articles of Teaching Principles" were enacted as the basis for education: 1) The principle of veneration of kami and love of country shall be obeyed; 2) The principle of heaven and the way of man shall be made clear; 3) The emperor must be reverently accepted and imperial instructions reverently defended.

In December the Great Teaching Academy (Taikyō-In) was opened in Tokyo as the central agency for education, and then in local districts smaller academies were opened. Teachers from both Shintō and Buddhism participated in the Great Teaching Academy. Here the strange scene appeared of Buddhist and Shintō priests together operating in distinctively Shintō fashion:

serving the *kami* in typical Shintō garb, offering up fish and fowl
on eight-legged tables, reciting Shintō prayers and clapping their
hands, explaining Shintō teachings. Thus the leading principle
of separation of Shintō and Buddhism ushered in by the Meiji
Restoration was reversed after but a few years. From February,
1873, the advantage of utilizing these teachers was recognized,
and therefore people from various walks of life—popular religious
leaders, ward headmen, local leaders, the local ruling class,
professional story-tellers, and comedians—were mobilized in
the indoctrination program.

The propagation of a Shintō-Buddhist amalgamation did not
actually produce results to the extent anticipated. The government's indoctrination movement, as shown in the Great Teaching
Academy's philosophy which provided its content, was a movement for enlightenment from above which included both a basic
creed and knowledge of industrial skills for the new age. Within
the Shintoistic education which formed the center of that movement, the Shintō doctrinal and organizational aspects were weak,
and the Shintō priests were no match for Buddhist priests in experience as propagators. Because local teaching academies were
agencies created without any consideration for popular belief, they
lacked support, and financial difficulties became severe. And in the
sphere of propagation the confrontation between Buddhist and
Shintō forces gradually increased.

The government already had actually abandoned the extreme
revivalism of the beginning of the Meiji Restoration, and raising
the slogan of "culture and enlightenment" they modernized
society and proceeded on the course of forming capitalism from
above. The prohibition of women at some sacred sites was abolished, and Buddhist priests became more free in marrying, eating
meat, and were no longer required to shave their hair. Under the
slogan of "washing away old customs," traditional practices were
discarded, and the modern thought and culture of Europe and
America came to be introduced and adopted. Among the leading
intellectuals of the Meiji Six Society (Meirokusha), such as Mori
Arinori and Nishi Amane, opinions were voiced calling for a modern state with freedom of religion, and for separation of government and religion; there were even people who advocated the
adoption of Christianity as a state religion.

Buddhism, now recovered from the attack of persecution, seized the situation and began to move with regard to freedom of religion and opposition to the Shintō-Buddhist amalgamation. It was the Shin sect which took the leadership of Buddhism's counterattack. Especially within the Honganji branch of the Shin sect, the advance of the sect into Hokkaidō was made in earnest, and it adopted Western culture positively, ardent in its organization's modernization. The leading priest of this branch, Shimaji Mokurai (1838–1911), had toured Europe and sent a petition to the government from Paris in which he criticized the "Three Articles of Teaching Principles." Arguing that the union of government and religion found in the propagation of a Shintō-Buddhist amalgamation violated freedom of religion and also did harm to patriotism, he requested the separation of government and religion. After returning to Japan, Shimaji united the four branches of the Shin sect and launched the movement to withdraw from the Great Teaching Academy, and in 1875 the withdrawal was finally realized. The Council of State abolished the propagation of Shintō-Buddhist amalgamation. The plan for a Ministry of Religious Education for national enlightenment on the basis of various religions fell through after just three years, and the Great Teaching Academy was dissolved. In November of the same year, the Ministry of Religious Education gave instructions to recognize freedom of religion, and two years later the Ministry of Religious Education itself was abolished, viewed even within the government as ineffective. The Shintō faction was aware of the movement to abolish the Great Teaching Academy and established the Shintō Office, creating an independent system in place of the academy.

At the same time that the government's religious policy began to fail, the activity of Tenri-kyō, Konkō-kyō, and such groups as the mountain pilgrimage associations again became active. However, the government proscribed healing of the sick by magical means and also exerted harsh oppression against the propagation of religions not officially recognized. The oppression of various popular religions was an initial step in the indoctrination for the emperor system, but it also attempted to control the practice of magic and exorcism which took advantage of the ignorance of the masses.

The government's religious policy required a major revision in order to ward off the advance of Christianity and, also, to place under control the most powerful religious groups—Buddhism and the new religions which developed by organizing the masses. The government allowed individual Buddhist sects to create their own teaching agencies and to propagate on the basis of their own doctrines; thereby the government created a system to control the individual sects by means of the chief priest. The Shintō Office became the agency of Shintō itself, apart from the government, and the pilgrimage associations and churches of popular religion and diverse origin came under the control of this office, thus legalizing their propagation.

3. The Reintroduction of Christianity

The new government, which immediately after the Meiji Restoration had continued the Tokugawa *bakufu's* ban on Christianity, was faced with protest from various Christian countries, and, considering the ban unsuitable for this era of "culture and enlightenment," in 1873 lifted it. In this situation, the government harbored deep anxieties as Christianity—being the background of the modern culture of the advanced capitalistic countries of Europe and America—was changed from a heretical sect to a foreign religion and began public propagation. The result was that Shintō and Buddhism again found themselves in company as forces rejecting foreign religion. Also the extraordinary sense of crisis concerning the attack on Christianity had lasting results for Buddhist propagation, and the accumulation of criticism against Christianity since Tokugawa times provided a broad base for Buddhism's considerable recovery of lost ground.

Bakufu and Early Meiji Persecution of Christianity

From the end of the Tokugawa period through early Meiji, Christianity was regarded by the traditional Japanese religious powers as a dreaded enemy. The reason for this is that Christianity formed the spiritual pillar of the European and American countries, which the government took as the model for advancing from above its modernization program of culture and enlightenment. Christian doctrine stood on principles completely different from Shintō and the Buddhist sects' semifeudal character, which was in the process of being adapted to the modern emperor system.

At the end of the Tokugawa period the reintroduction of Christianity into Japan as a banned religion was initiated by Catholic missions. The Catholics already since Tempō times (1830–44) had entered Korea and the Ryūkyū Islands and were advancing their preparations for propagation in Japan. In 1844, the French priest T.A. Forçade (1816–85) of the Société des Missions Etrangères de Paris arrived at Naha in Okinawa via a French warship and was arrested, but a little later the French priest B.T. Petitjean (1829–84) arrived there. This French mission cooperated in the administration of France's Asian colonies, and because it obtained widespread results in the propagation of Catholicism within Indochina, it planned as its next goal the propagation of Catholicism in Japan with the backing of French power.

In 1858 when the Franco-Japanese commercial treaty was concluded, P.S. Girard (1821–67) was appointed to head the diocese of Japan and landed in Japan immediately after the official opening of Japan. Girard was to be the chaplain attached to the French embassy, and in 1862 built a Catholic chapel at Yokohama. This was about two and a half centuries since all churches in Japan had been banned by the *bakufu*. This chapel was for the use of foreign residents, but people called it the "Jesus temple" (*yasodera*) and came to see it, and listened to the sermons which the priests delivered in faltering Japanese.

In 1865, Petitjean built a chapel next to the French Consulate in Ōura in Nagasaki for French residents. This chapel was a church built in the traditional European style, with a lofty steeple and stained glass. People of this area called it the "French temple," and they were awe-struck with the beauty and foreignness of the new chapel. After the completion of the chapel, a score of peasants, hidden Christians of Urakami who had preserved their faith and resisted the prohibition of Christianity, secretly visited the chapel. When the peasants entered the chapel, three of the older peasant women quietly approached Petitjean and said that "our own hearts are the same as yours," and asked where the statue of Santa Maria[1] was. When the surprised Petitjean took them by the hand and showed them the statue of Mary enshrined within the chapel, the peasants knelt before it and expressed their devotion.

---

[1] Because of the prominent role of Portuguese priests in the propagation of Catholicism in the sixteenth century, early Japanese Christians and the later hidden Christians (kakure Kirishitan) borrowed many Portuguese terms, such as Santa Maria.

The history of the martyrdom of Japanese Christianity from the sixteenth century on was known in detail in Europe. Petitjean knew that Christianity had once prospered in Japan but thought that during two hundred years as a forbidden religion Christianity had completely died out. Now Petitjean recognized that these Japanese peasants were without a doubt Christian believers, and thanking God for this miracle, he notified Rome. Christianity finally was restored, and Urakami Christian families severed their ties with parish Buddhist temples and revolted against the temple registration system. The Nagasaki administrative office of the *bakufu* attempted to suppress the movement, but before long the *bakufu* collapsed. The new Meiji government ordered Inoue Kaoru and Ōkuma Shigenobu (under the nobleman Sawa Nobuyoshi, who was appointed as the Nagasaki Court Governor) to Nagasaki and immediately set out on a major suppression. Inoue proclaimed: "The whole village of Urakami should be reduced to barren earth," thus showing his fierce determination. In June, 1869, the government opened an imperial conference and decided to sentence all the Urakami Christians to exile. In this fashion the thorough religious oppression of the exile of 3,109 Urakami Christians was carried out. This is what they call the fourth fall of Urakami, and it was to be the last of a series of persecutions against Urakami Christians.

Secret Protestant Missionary Work

Immediately after its establishment, the new government made an official announcement of prohibition of the "heretical religion Christianity," but the ambassadors of Christian countries jointly protested the labeling of Christianity as a heretical religion. The government feared the diplomatic disadvantages and rewrote the official announcement, posting it with two separate paragraphs, one for the prohibition of Christianity, and one for the prohibition of heretical religions. The Urakami Christians, ordered to exile, were encouraged to abandon their faith and all the believers were scattered through 21 feudal domains. The believers were advised with flattery to renounce their religion and also were tortured, such that one-fifth of them died in exile. In Tsuwano domain, the home of the Hirata school of Shintō, cruel torture and investigation were carried out. The Urakami incident was also subjected to the loud denunciation of the Christian countries.

About this time, from the end of the Tokugawa period, Protestantism, which was secretly promoting its missionary work, continued to spread its teaching in the midst of the new government's oppression. From the end of the Tokugawa period until early Meiji, missionary work was being promoted by missionaries of French Catholicism and of the Greek and Russian Orthodox churches. The missionaries of various Protestant denominations from the United States, Canada, England, and Holland came to Japan. Since the end of the Tokugawa period, they had used China and the Ryūkyū Islands as their base and promoted the translation of the Bible, and after the opening of Japan, Americans and others gradually came to Japan. The missionaries who came at the end of the Tokugawa period began their work at Nagasaki and Kanagawa (Yokohama). At Nagasaki, J. Liggins (1829–1912) and C. M. Williams (1829–1910) of the American Episcopal Church lived in the temple Sōfuku-ji and waited for the legalization of missionary work. G. H. F. Verbeck (1830–98) of the (American) Dutch Reformed Church taught Western subjects in the domain school of Saga, and before long a number of the domain's *samurai* were baptized. In Kanagawa, J. C. Hepburn (1815–1911) of the American Presbyterian Church, while treating Japanese patients as a physician, opened a private school and taught young students. S. R. Brown (1810–80), D. B. Simmons (1834–89), and J. H. Ballagh (1832–1920) of the (American) Dutch Reformed Church and J. Goble (1827–98) of the American Baptist Church also came to Kanagawa. Because open missionary work was forbidden under the government order, these missionaries taught English and other subjects along with Christianity in their uncertain Japanese to young students. With the cooperation of some Japanese people, they managed to translate the Bible into Japanese. In 1865, the physician Yano Mototaka (?–1865) was baptized by Ballagh in Kanagawa, becoming the first Japanese Protestant.

In the early years of the Meiji era, young descendants of *samurai* who because of the collapse of the feudal system were seeking a new way of life, gathered around the missionaries. With their Confucian upbringing, these young people were able to respect the missionaries' strict attitude toward life. They approached Christianity through a deep attraction to the advanced civilization of Europe and America. Not only did Christianity open the young people's eyes to the advanced culture of Europe and America, but also the youths, through belief in Christ, believed in original sin; being together with their savior they acquired the courage to live with strength in the severe changes of the new era. In violation of the new government's order, in the early years of Meiji, Ferris Girls' School, Kyōritsu Gakuen, and other Protestant women's educational institutions were founded.

Starting in 1872, a prayer meeting with some thirty young participants was begun among the students studying the Bible at Ballagh's English school in Yokohama. The prayer meeting was planned for one week, but because of the intensity of the enthusiasm among the youths who gathered, the meeting lasted over a month. Nine received baptism as a result, and in March, 1872, the Church of Christ in Japan, Nihon Kirisuto Kōkai, a Presbyterian church, was founded by this group in Yokohama. This was the first Japanese Protestant church. Such groups as the Dutch Reformed Church and the American Presbyterian Church assisted the Church of Christ in Japan, but it assumed an independent and self-governing framework in accordance with the Japanese believers and belonged to no individual denomination.

By this time, the ban on Christianity was almost anachronistic, but the Ministry of Religions Education continued to use the prohibition order as a pretext to spy on the movements of Christians; people were imprisoned, such as the case of Ichikawa Einosuke (1835–72) and his wife, because they were said to have aided foreign missionaries and to have spread Christianity in Kobe and Nagasaki. Shintō and Buddhist factions loudly warned of the dangers of this foreign religion, and with the revival of the anti-Christian literature of the Tokugawa period, books denouncing Christianity were printed one after another.

In 1871, a mission of Ambassador Extraordinary Iwakura Tomomi visited Europe for about a year and a half; wherever it went, this mission received the people's protests against the Japanese government's persecution of Christianity.

Protestantism in Kumamoto and Sapporo

In February, 1873, the government finally withdrew the official orders on the prohibition of Christianity and the prohibition of heretical religions. This meant that while barely preserving the dignity of the government, it gave tacit approval to the propagation of Christianity. With the lifting of the ban, Christianity in Japan welcomed a new era. Protestantism entered into public activities fourteen years after foreign missionaries first came to Japan at the end of the Tokugawa period. This was the year the Church of Christ in Japan was established at Tokyo, and in the following year branches of this church were formed at Kobe and Osaka. From this time the propagation of the newly arrived denominations, such as Methodist, began. In Tokyo, the Presbyterians formed the Presbyterian Church in Japan; and the Kansai branch of the Church of Christ in Japan came under influence of the American Congregational Church.

The Japanese Protestant movement, though still small, centered around such people as Oshikawa Masayoshi (1849–1928), Honda Yōichi (1848–1912), Okuno Masatsuna (1823–1920), Uemura Masahisa (1858–1925), and Ibuka Kajinosuke (1854–1940). Among the leading Japanese believers of that time, there were many who entered the faith through a national consciousness, trying through Christianity to make Japan a wealthy and powerful nation not inferior to European and American countries, interpreting Christianity through Confucian ethics. For these leaders, the dominant idea was that churches should be managed by Japanese hands, and that foreign aid should not be accepted. They held an attitude toward life based on a modern citizen morality, and there were many who rejected government invitations and chose to remain among the people in order to devote their lives to preaching. For them, faith and patriotism were actually one; they did not realize that a modern ethics guided by Christianity was essentially incompatible with a national morality of loyalty and patriotism that held up the modern emperor system and patriarchal familism.

In 1874 Niijima Jō (1843–90) returned to Japan. Niijima had secretly left Japan for the United States in the late Tokugawa period,[2]

---

[2] During this period, Japanese people were forbidden by law to leave the country.

received baptism, and studied Christian theology. He was the child of a *samurai* of the Annaka domain of Kōzuke (Gumma Prefecture). He went to the treaty port of Hakodate and from there stowed away on a ship to America, but with his determination to devote his life to Japanese missionary work, after an absence of ten years he returned to Japan. At first Niijima conducted his mission work in his native region of Annaka, but he moved to the Kansai area in the following year because the Congregational Church to which he belonged was chiefly active there. Niijima was determined to build a Christian school, and in the face of fierce opposition from temples and shrines, in 1875 he opened the Dōshisha English School with a mere eight students.

In January, 1876, 35 students of a Western school in Kumamoto, under the inspiration of the American instructor Captain L.L. Janes (1838–1909) climbed Mt. Hanaoka to announce their conversion to Christianity by repeating a pledge that referred to faith and patriotism as one entity. In the fall of the same year the Kumamoto advocates of practical learning who, starting with the Western schools, were in the process of absorbing the technical culture of the West, were opposed by more than 170 discontented conservative warriors. These reactionary forces called for an anti-foreign restoration based on Shintō and provoked the riot of the Divine Wind League (Shimpūren).

The Western schools were, as a consequence, closed, and the young group of believers, known as the "Kumamoto Band," moved to Dōshisha. Among the Kumamoto Band were Kozaki Hiromichi (1856–1938), Ebina Danjō (1856–1937), and Miyagawa Tsuneteru (1857–1936), the future leaders of the Congregational Church, and the Tokutomi brothers (Sohō, 1863–1957, and Roka, 1868–1927). Dōshisha students, including the Kumamoto Band, nurtured under Niijima, became a significant force in the development of Christianity during the Meiji era.

In 1876, Kuroda Kiyotaka, the commissioner for the development of Hokkaidō, invited W. S. Clark (1826–86), the president of Massachusetts Agricultural College, as principal of Sapporo School of Agriculture. Clark was an ardent Christian and persuaded Kuroda to permit Christian education for the students. Clark left Japan after being in office for only eight months, but the Christian spirit that he left behind made a deep impression on his students. Soon after Clark's return to the United States, Uchimura Kanzō (1861–1930) and Nitobe Inazō (1862–1933), both students of the Sapporo School, received baptism in the Methodist Church. Thus, Yokohama, Kumamoto, and Sapporo became the three great centers of Japanese Protestantism.

4. State Shintō and Sect Shintō

Following the Meiji Restoration, Shintō increased its strength by promoting the unity of ritual and government, and nationalization of Shintō. However, due to a change in religious policy by the dissolution of the Great Teaching Academy and the abolition of the Ministry of Religious Education, antagonism and rivalry gradually intensified among the various groups of Restoration Shintō. Shintō was not deeply rooted in the folk religious life of the people. In 1876, the Shintō Kurozumi sect (later Kurozumi-kyō) and the Shintō Shūsei sect, which already possessed powerful voluntary organizations and which had contributed financially to the Great Teaching Academy movement, became independent of the Shintō Office. The Shintō Shūsei sect was based on the strongly Confucian-colored Shintō interpretation advanced by the imperialist Nitta Kuniteru (1815–1902), but in the actual strength of teaching, the main force was occupied by the mountain pilgrimage associations, such as Fuji and Ontake, of which Nitta was the leader. Within Shintō, the period of upheaval of the Meiji Restoration was over, and with the retreat of the Restoration Shintō faction, the dispute surrounding the *kami* dedicated at the Shintō Office became a turning point in Shintō.

The *kami* venerated in the shrine of the Great Teaching Academy (which was built as the central shrine of Shintō) were the three *kami* of creation—Amenominakanushi, Takamimusubi, and Kamimusubi—and a fourth *kami*, the imperial ancestral *kami* Amaterasu Ōmikami. After the abolition of the Great Teaching Academy, it was arranged that the sanctuary be transferred to the *yōhaisho*[1] of Ise Shrine within the Shintō Office. Senge Takatomi

---

[1] Remote worship site; often a site rather distant from a shrine was designated so that people could perform worship without actually traveling to the shrine.

41

(1845–1918), the head of Izumo Taisha-kyō,[2] added Ōkuninushi, the main *kami* of Izumo Taisha (Grand Shrine of Izumo), and insisted on these five as the main deities. In the Shintō pantheon, Ōkuninushi controlled the realm of the dead (*yūmeikai*), and this *kami* would be able to assure spiritual peace to the people. In opposition to this, the chief priest Tanaka Yoritsune (1836–97) of Ise Shrine and the Shintoist Ise sect insisted on four chief *kami* and did not yield. In the Tokugawa period, Izumo Taisha attracted a wide base of belief, especially in western Japan from such people as farmers, fishermen, sailors, merchants, and craftsmen. This was due to the influence of Izumo priests and shamans as *kami* of this-worldly benefit and love charms. After the Meiji Restoration, they organized the Izumo Taisha Piety Association, and formed a powerful force in the Shintō world as the Izumo sect, but the Izumo Taisha rested on a doctrinal viewpoint fundamentally different from the Shintō centered at Ise, and opposed the Shintoist Ise sect. The dispute over the dedicated *kami* was a major one that split the Shintō world in two, and a decision was sought from the government. In December, 1880, by order of the emperor a Conference of Shintō was convened in Tokyo, and as a result of the conference they agreed to respect the judgment of the emperor concerning both dedicated *kami* and the selections of the Shintō superintendent priest. Emperor Meiji considered all the divinities venerated within the imperial court as the dedicated *kami* of the Shintō Office, and appointed the imperial prince Arisugawa-no-miya Taruhito (1835–95) as the head of Shintō. The dispute within the Shintō organizations was resolved through the mediation of the emperor, but the immaturity and frailty of Shintō doctrine was exposed from both within and without. The necessity of separating general religious activities from the function of shrines as national agencies was also emphasized as a result.

Shintō's Nonreligious Function

The government established a policy of distinguishing Shintō from religion in general; it prohibited Shintō priests of imperial

[2] Izumo Taisha-kyō, one of the thirteen groups of Sect Shintō.

(Kampeisha) and national shrines (Kokuheisha) from doubling as moral instructors, and from being associated with burial rites. This removed the core of religious activities from Shintō and gave it a special status beyond its religious function, one of performing national rituals. This was a measure for the purpose of separating religion from ritual. The government, facing the demand for freedom of religion and for separation of government and religion, set up a framework in which Shintō was not a religion. And by placing rituals within shrines and returning to the emperor the supreme authority for rituals, unity of ritual and government was maintained. However, the fact that this forced the specific religion of Shintō upon the nation as a state ritual—with all levels of Shintō priests as an authoritative religious bureaucracy—clearly contradicted the framework of a modern nation. The modern imperial system of government, as long as it used the emperor's religious authority as the most powerful ideological tool for control of the people, felt the necessity of both the anachronistic emperor system and its policy of unity of government and religion. The government's argument of the nonreligious character of shrines was the sophistry used for rationalizing this contradiction.

After 1882, in accordance with the policy of separating ritual from religion, various religious groups became independent of the Shintō Office: Taisha-kyō (later called Izumo Ōyashiro-kyō), Jingū-kyō (the voluntary association of Ise Shrine, later called Jingū Hōsaikai), Taisei-kyō, Shinshū-kyō, Fusō-kyō (linked with belief in Mount Fuji), Jikkō-kyō (which Shibata Hanamori, 1809–90, had developed out of the tradition of belief in Mount Fuji), and Mitake-kyō (linked with belief in Mount Ontake, later called Ontake-kyō). The Shintō Office in 1886 became an independent religion under the name of Shintō (or Shintō Honkyoku, later Shintō Taikyō). In 1894, independent existence was recognized for Misogi-kyō (the successor to Inoue Masakane's Tohokami Shintō, which was formed into a group after the Meiji Restoration) and Shinri-kyō (or Kannagi-be Shintō). These religions, originally belonging to the Shintō Office, organized the doctrines of Shintō lines and were officially recognized as independent religions; they are called Sect Shintō (Kyōha Shintō, or Sectarian Shintō or Religious Shintō). Sect Shintō, in the meaning of Shintō as a religion, was placed on a lower dimension than the Shrine Shintō (State

Shintō) which was the state ritual; together with Buddhism, it occupied the status of an officially recognized religion under the system of State Shintō.

Recognition of Tenri-kyō and Konkō-kyō

In the 1880s, Tenri-kyō, with the Osaka region as its center, spread throughout the country. The founder Nakayama Miki was repeatedly persecuted, and in her writing *Ofudesaki* she scathed the government for interfering with the work of the *kami*. The police, under the pretext of saving the people from Tenri-kyō, repeated their provocation and suppression of this religion, and Nakayama was subjected to 18 arrests. In 1882, the stone *kanrodai*,[3] kept indoors as the supreme object of veneration in the center of holy grounds, was destroyed and carried away by the police; Nakayama's indignation toward the government authorities was such that she ceased her literary work, *Ofudesaki* ("tip of the pen"), which she had begun in 1869. Nakayama wrote the *Kōki*, Tenri-kyō's distinctive creation myth of man and the universe, and established a doctrine of the providence of salvation for the entire world by Tenri-Ō-no-Mikoto. Tenri-kyō was established before the formation of State Shintō ideology, and during the Tokugawa period and the beginning of the Meiji era had formed a doctrine centering on this world and the salvation of humankind. Emperor worship played no role in it. The *Kōki* myth, which explained the beginning of the world by the swimming of many fish within a muddy ocean, also offered a system different from the imperial myth, which justified the political control of the emperor. For this reason, under State Shintō, the existence of the *Kōki* was the clincher that always threatened Tenri-kyō with the crime of *lèse majesté*.

In the 1880s, Tenri-kyō and such popular religions as Konkō-kyō, Remmon-kyō (linked to Hokke Shintō), and Maruyama-kyō (linked to belief in Mount Fuji), spread throughout the country. Tenri-kyō and Konkō-kyō are typical popular religions that formed at the end of the Tokugawa period and beginning of Meiji.

---

[3] *Kanrodai*, interpreted by Tenri-kyō publications as "a sacred stand with a vessel on it for receiving *kanro*, or heavenly dew," symbolizes the place where human beings were created.

The development of the remarkable religious strength of these two religions at this time took place against the background of the social upheaval characteristic of the adoption of capitalism from above: due to the forces in the early stages of the accumulation of capital, the ruin of middle- and lower-class farmers and the reorganization of farm villages was taking place throughout the country. Tenri-kyō and Konkō-kyō, through their doctrine of salvation, were able to organize on a large scale the farmers, merchants, and industrialists who directly experienced the crisis.

Konkō-kyō, too, in the midst of government persecution spread from the Osaka, southwestern Honshū, and northern Kyūshū regions to Tokyo. Under its policy of suppressing newly formed popular religions, the government manipulated various religions and brought them under its control, planning the mobilization for edification of the people based on State Shintō. Both Tenri-kyō's founder Nakayama Miki and Konkō-kyō's founder Konkō Daijin suffered the consequences of oppression due to the government's aim of trying to control belief with political authority, for throughout their lifetimes, both continued to reject the course of legalization and official recognition through subordination to State Shintō. Nakayama left the testament that "the decision of the heart comes first, before the law," and taught that faith is superior to secular authority. However, in the 1880s by the time Tenri-kyō and Konkō-kyō had grown into nationwide religious bodies, in order to avoid the governmental oppression and to legalize their missionary work, these religions prepared doctrines to conform with State Shintō and requested official recognition as individual sects of Sect Shintō. After these two religions became affiliated with Shintō Honkyoku, they continued to serve national interests and received official recognition as independent sects, Konkō-kyō in 1900 and Tenri-kyō in 1908.

Sect Shintō, with the recognition of Tenri-kyō, numbered 14 religious groups, but later Jingū-kyō, upon the institution of civil law, became a legal foundation (under the name Jingū Hōsaikai), and usually Sect Shintō is referred to as having 13 sects. Sect Shintō was given privileges and protection as an officially recognized religion, and the leaders of each group of Sect Shintō received treatment as imperial appointees. Sect Shintō's main strength was found in: the various groups, such as Kurozumi-kyō, Tenri-kyō, and Konkō-kyō which arose out of the area stretching from western Honshū to the Kyoto-Osaka area; the various mountain religion groups, which were descended from Shugendō;[4] and also the various groups of Kannagara-no-Michi (Shintō) which entered the fold of State Shintō. Most of these religions, both in doctrine and tradition, differed in character from the Shintō which the government established as the state religion. In order to strengthen and solidify State Shintō, a religion that lacked popular support and recognition, various popular religious groups of late Tokugawa and early Meiji were brought under control and organized into Sect Shintō, to be used as support for the State Shintō system.

The Development of Protestantism

The Christian missionary work at the time of the Freedom and Popular Rights Movement in the 1870s and 1880s steadily bore fruit, and churches were established in regional cities one after another. In 1877, the Church of Christ in Japan and the Presbyterian Church, which was strong in the area surrounding Tokyo, united to form the United Church of Christ in Japan, Nihon Kirisuto Itchi Kyōkai (later the Church of Christ in Japan, Nihon Kirisuto Kyōkai) with a membership of 623. The next year at Tokyo the first Japanese Christian Believers Friendship Conference was held, and representatives from 12 areas participated. The same year the number of believers in the whole country had increased to over 1,600, and the missionaries, in defiance of surrounding resistance and oppression, expanded their missionary work from the cities to farm villages. Activity opposing the government's land tax reform and calling for the establishment of representatives elected by the people, developed into the nationwide Freedom and Popular Rights Movement and was growing in size, but it was Christianity, which preached faith in Jesus Christ and modern citizen ethics, that became a powerful counterattack to the Confucian "familism" and State Shintō's

---

[4] Shugendō is the official name for the organization of *yamabushi* which once flourished with headquarters on many mountains; it was formally proscribed by the government in 1872, but several centers have been reestablished after 1945.

edification of the people. Protestantism won ardent believers among the warrior class, landowners, intellectuals, women, and students; and when Honda Yōichi (1848–1912), pastor of the Hirosaki Church, became a representative for the petition to establish a national assembly, there appeared many Christians who became local representatives and were active for the cause of freedom and popular rights. In 1880, the Tokyo YMCA was founded, and in its magazine *Rikugo Zasshi* published rebuttals to the criticism of Christianity by Fukuzawa Yukichi (1834–1901), Taguchi Ukichi (1855–1905), and Inoue Tetsujirō (1855–1944).

In 1882, the number of Protestant churches was 93, the number of believers more than 4,300. The next year in Tokyo the third Believers' Friendship Conference was held, and the intensity of the faith of the assembled believers was seen as they prayed in earnest, with some believers even crying out. This revival spread throughout the country, and for over a year it took place among the the students of Dōshisha. The Freedom and Popular Rights Movement waned, and with the revision of unequal treaties, a new phase of Westernization was ushered in. Various Christian denominations grew active in missionary work, and there arose a strong tendency to establish denominations affiliated with foreign missions in Japan. Even after Christianity had passed through this revival period, it continued to develop, bolstered by more than 10,000 believers.

In February, 1889, the Meiji Constitution was promulgated. According to the Constitution, missionary activities of three religions—Shintō (Sect Shintō), Buddhism, and Christianity—were officially recognized; at the same time it was established that the emperor was of divine character as a "manifest *kami*," and that he had religious authority as holder of sovereignty over ritual.

On the day of the promulgation of the Constitution, the Minister of Education, Mori Arinori, regarded as the central figure in the movement for Westernization, was assassinated by a group of Shintō priests from Ise Shrine, and the next year at the First High School there occurred the *lèse majesté* incident of Uchimura Kanzō when he did not pay homage to the imperial signature on the Rescript on Education. It was the next year that Kume Kunitake was forced from his position at Tokyo Imperial University because of his essay "Shintō Is the Survival of a Cult of Heaven" (*Shintō wa Saiten no Kozoku*). Ultranationalist groups of Shintō and Buddhist origins were founded, all of which advocated patriotism and loyalty to the emperor and which began an assault on Christianity. Among these were Yamaoka Tesshū (1836–88) and Torio Tokuan (1847–1905) of the Nihon Kokkyō Daidōsha (Society for Establishing the Great Way as the National Religion of Japan);[5] the Kannagara Gakkai (leader of the Shintō schools); and Ōuchi Seiran (1845–1918) of the Sonnō Hōbutsu Daidōdan (Revere the Emperor and Serve the Buddha Federation).

The general tendency of Japanese Christians was to greet the promulgation of the Constitution as the legal recognition of missionary work. However, the religious principles on which the emperor system was based were basically incompatible with Christianity, causing a head-on clash between education based on the emperor system and religion in general. The criticism of politics and society that Christianity had expressed in the first decade of Meiji receded, in line with the policy of Japanese Christianity; throughout the Meiji era the powerful denominations, such as the Church of Christ in Japan, the Congregational, Methodist, and Anglican churches carried out educational, cultural, and social work. Protestantism was supported widely among the intellectuals advocating modernization, and successful endeavors were made in the fields of thought and literature and by the acceptance of modern culture and modern citizen morality. However, the general trend gradually leaned toward support for the modern emperor system and nationalism.

Growth of New Religions

Meanwhile, within Tenri-kyō (which had expanded with its doctrines of magical this-worldly benefit and the quest for realization of a theocracy), after the death of its founder in 1887 the major disciple Iburi Izō (1833–1907) published the *Osashizu*, a collection of Nakayama's and his own teachings, and became the new leader. During the lifetime of the founder, Tenri-kyō had

[5] Great Way, Daidō, means Confucianism, Shintō, and Buddhism.

become affiliated with Shintō Honkyoku and had achieved a tentative legalization. Its support for the government and decrease of criticism of the authorities enabled Tenri-kyō to develop its strength as a religion. Konkō-kyō spread throughout the country as a faith of this-worldy benefits, such as faith-healing and success in business. At the same time, Maruyama-kyō, linked to belief in Mount Fuji, displayed its organizational strength, primarily in the Tokyo vicinity and in the area between Tokyo and Nagoya with a membership numbering several hundred thousand. Also, Remmon-kyō, a Shintō transformation of faith in the Lotus Sutra, moved into Tokyo in 1882 and developed in western Japan and Tokyo.

Maruyama-kyō

Maruyama-kyō is a peasant religion of "mountain religion" derivation which was founded by Itō Rokurobei (1829–94), a landowner of Inada Noborito of Kanagawa Prefecture. Itō was a pilgrim guide who led the Maruyama pilgrim association, a group affiliated with the Fuji pilgrim association. He was called a "living *kami* ascetic," and engaged in missionary work by means of faith-healing but met with suppression under the program for edification of the people, and in order to legalize his missionary work he became affiliated with Fusō-kyō. After establishing its strength as a religion, Maruyama-kyō separated from Fusō-kyō and became affiliated with Shintō Honkyoku. According to Maruyama-kyō's doctrine, if man exerts his "own spirit"[6] that he was granted by his "father and mother" (the traditional *kami* of creation and growth in the Fuji pilgrim association), and lives out his life cheerfully in mutual harmony, then man can "return home" to the source of the *kami*. According to this faith men throughout the world will find good fortune, with the realization of the ideal world of peace and prosperity. In the tradition of the Fuji pilgrim associations there is faith in Miroku Bosatsu (Maitreya Bodhisattva), the Buddhist savior, and in the doctrine of Maruyama-kyō, too, we can trace the this-worldly world renewal rooted in peasant life, and pacifist themes. In 1885, one group of Maruyama-kyō followers within Shizuoka Prefecture was led by the peasant pilgrim leader Nishigaya

---

6 "Own spirit," *ichibu no kokoro;* the spirit or soul granted every person by the *kami*.

Heishirō and advocated a revived anti-war world renewal. A large number of followers from farm villages in both Shizuoka and Nagano Prefectures, believing that this world would change and that they would become feudal lords, became involved in this movement, which was suppressed by the police. During the Sino-Japanese War of 1894 through 1895, there was draft evasion and anti-war activity among Maruyama-kyō believers.

Remmon-kyō

Remmon-kyō was a religion founded in 1868 by Shimamura Mitsu (1831–1914), the wife of a merchant in Kokura, Kyūshū. This was about the same time that faith in the Lotus Sutra was undergoing doctrinal revision under the influence of State Shintō. From about 1880 and continuing through 1895, Remmon-kyō increased its strength as a religion, first in Tokyo, southwestern Honshū, and northern Kyūshū, and then nationwide, through this-worldly benefits, such as faith-healing, and acquired several hundred thousand followers. The believers worshiped by reciting *"ji no myōhō, nam myōhō rengekyō"*[7] five times and clapping their hands before the altar. In rituals they used the Nakatomi purification and the Great Purification from Shintō. *"Ji no myōhō"* comes from the fact that in the system of the Lotus Sutra they distinguish between *ri* (noumenon or truth) as the abstract theory and *ji* (phenomenon or the relative) as the concrete actuality; thus *ji* refers to the actually realized ultimate of the Lotus Sutra. The founder was a living *kami*, and this religion taught that if one believed in Venerable Ji no Myōhō and drank sacred water, then there would be no need for doctors or medicine to cure diseases or illnesses, and all this-worldly benefits would be available. In the face of a cholera epidemic in Tokyo, Remmon-kyō spread the message that cholera could be cured with sacred water, and many people became believers. In order to legalize their missionary work, they became affiliated with Taisei-kyō, but because of their faith-healing they were subject to severe suppression and interference from the police. Remmon-kyō was also criticized as a heretical sect by intellectuals, newspapers, and established religions. Its strength

---

[7] *Nam* (or *namu*) *myōhō rengekyō* is the familiar recitation taken from Nichiren Buddhism meaning literally "Hail to the Wonderful Law of the Lotus Sutra"; *ji no myōhō* is a phrase added by Remmon-kyō.

as a religion weakened quickly at the turn of the century, and after that all groups associated with this religion became extinct. From the disappearance of Remmon-kyō we may draw two conclusions: social criticism toward faith-healing and other magical practices was a significant factor; however, the fact that its doctrine of Shintō-Buddhist syncretism of "Lotus Sutra Shintō" could not find room for development within State Shintō's system of religious control was also cause for Remmon-kyō's extinction.

II. Difficulties in Modernization

1900s-1910s

5. The New Buddhist Movement

The Sino-Japanese War began in 1894 out of the struggle for the Korean market, when Japan, with its aim of moving from the Korean peninsula into the Chinese continent, touched off war with China. During the war, Nishi Honganji (a prominent Pure Land sect) and all Buddhist sects, upholding Buddhism's reputation as "protector of the country," cooperated in the war by sending chaplains to accompany the army. Japan devoted its national strength to a full-scale overseas war almost without historical precedent, and the government advocated the spirit of "loyalty to ruler and patriotism." Worship at Shintō shrines permeated the life of the people through prayers for military success and protection during battle.

Due to the intervention of Russia, France, and Germany, Japan returned to Manchu China the Liaotung Peninsula, which it had acquired in the treaty following the Sino-Japanese War. The Japanese government concentrated the anti-foreign sentiment fanned by the three countries' intervention into the slogan of "perseverance and endurance," and proceeded with the preparations for the forthcoming war against Russia. Throughout the Sino-Japanese War, Japanese capitalism strengthened its militaristic character even more. The industrial revolution advanced on a large scale, especially in the field of heavy industry, as well as in the spinning industry and silk manufacture, which up to this time had been the major industries. In 1902, Japan entered into the Anglo-Japanese Alliance and opposed the southern expansion of imperial Russia. In Japan's competition with imperial Russia over the right to control Korea and Manchuria, Japan received the support of the United Kingdom and the United States, and in February of 1904, with a surprise attack on the Russian fleet at Inchon and Port Arthur, Japan entered the Russo-Japanese War.

At the time of the Russo-Japanese War, Japanese capitalism was undergoing full-scale development. The working class was born, made up chiefly from industrial workers who drifted away from farm villages and were attracted to the industrial areas of large metropolises. New social problems emerged in the process in the form of labor problems, and these, along with tenant uprisings in the villages, were among the difficulties which in this era took on a new dimension. Japan's modernization process was distinct in that it preserved in part a feudalistic character while taking as its keynote anti-foreign and nationalistic principles. The social movements of the time became associated with the growing influence of socialist and anarchist thought.

Signs of Buddhism's Modernization

Learning from the example of (Protestant) Christianity which from the start had dealt with social problems and worked in educational fields, and also in order to counteract the influence of Christianity, Buddhist circles gradually came to show concern for social work, and a modern educational system with separate grade levels was soon founded.

Buddhism weathered the storm of persecution at the beginning of Meiji, succeeded in adapting to the modern emperor system, and reestablished its position as Japan's greatest religious force. However, this rapid recovery of Buddhism, on the other hand, resulted in its preserving its premodern, feudalistic character. Every sect of Buddhism had depended on the parish system of the Tokugawa period, and in everything emphasized ancestor worship; the family still functioned as the main link for Buddhist funeral and memorial rites. Buddhism built up a stable foundation from both urban and rural populations, which comprised the overwhelming percentage of society.

Around the turn of the century, the more progressive Buddhists wanted to do away with this old Buddhism and strove for the modernization of Buddhism. This developed into a movement for the reformation of religious organizations and for a new Buddhism.

One example of this was the formation of the Buddhist Pure

Believers Friends Association (later renamed the New Buddhism Friends Association) in 1899. This group began as a *hansei-kai* (literally, self-examination society) which ordinary adherents of Nishi Honganji formed, gathering together enthusiastic Buddhists, such as Furukawa Isamu (Rōsen, 1871–99), Sakaino Kōyō (1871–1933), Takashima Beihō (1875–1949), Sugimura Jūō (Sojinkan, 1872–1945), and Watanabe Kaikyoku (1872–1933). Their call for a confrontation with the old Buddhism in free debate and their advocacy of a modern new Buddhism with social concern caused much debate both within and without Buddhist circles. The title of the association emulated the Puritans and can be said to have aimed at the establishment of a religion of a modern citizens' society. It even kept up a close relationship with socialists and (Christian) Unitarians.

In the following year, the spiritual movement Kōkōdō (literally, the active den) developed from the reform movement of the Shinshū Ōtani sect (Higashi Honganji), centering on Kiyozawa Manshi (1863–1903) and such figures as Sasaki Gesshō (1875–1926), Tada Kanae, and Akegarasu Haya (1877–1954). Its emphasis was to reject the course of "state Buddhism" under imperialist state authority; instead it pursued the individual awakening from self to non-self and the higher self, and from one's private self to the social self. Kiyozawa taught the way of saving the modern self according to Buddhism in his phrase "simply enslave yourself to Buddha." Buddhism became a very personal religion under Kōkōdō, a philosophy that could cope with modern society, and the movement exerted a great influence on the Buddhist world as well as on intellectuals.

The fact that people turned to Buddhism in the confrontation with social problems, and that Buddhism's modernization was advocated through the establishment of a modern self as a Buddhist, pointed out the contradiction involving every sect that existed peaceably within the framework of State Shintō. In the scholarly studies of every sect, they inherited the tradition of Sanskrit studies from the priest Jiun of the Tokugawa period. However, there was controversy surrounding the foundation of religious truth as expressed in Murakami Senjō's (1851–1929) publication "The Theory That Mahayana Is Not the Buddha's Teachings," (1901) which reflected the results of modern European studies on

Buddhism. Because the work expressed his own views about Buddhism, Murakami was forced to give up the Buddhist priesthood. In 1905 Itō Shōshin (1876–1963) of the Shinshū Ōtani sect founded Mugaen (literally, the Non-Self Garden) which taught a life of service. In the same year Nishida Tenkō (1872–1968), having been strongly influenced by Ninomiya Sontoku's teaching of repayment of virtue[1] and by Leo Tolstoy, and pained by the contradictions of society, sought a true way in human life and confined himself for meditation in Aizen in his birthplace Nagahama, Shiga Prefecture. Suddenly he heard the crying voice of a baby, and he was enlightened to the innocent and helpless character of human life and founded Ittōen, a movement featuring elements common to various religious traditions. In the last years of Meiji there also appeared Buddhist anarchists, such as Uchiyama Gudō (1874–1911) who was involved in the Taigyaku Incident in 1910, in which several hundred socialists and anarchists were arrested on trumped up charges on a plot to assassinate Emperor Meiji.

After the Russo-Japanese War, the sects of Buddhism, including about 72,000 temples and 53,000 priests and nuns, became increasingly nationalistic and actively promoted their overseas missionary work in Korea, China, and Siberia, and extending as far as Hawaii, North America, and South America. Ōtani Kōzui (1876–1948) of Nishi Honganji, while still a student in London, planned an expedition to Central Asia, and in 1902 led the expeditionary group himself and explored the regions of western China. Later, when Ōtani attained the highest rank in Nishi Honganji, he attempted to modernize the sect. In a manner that might be considered typical of a powerful religious leader, he invested in large enterprises but only caused the ruin of the organization's finances, retiring ten years after his inauguration. At the same time, Higashi Honganji also fell into a financial crisis. These two incidents made a lasting impression on society of the premodern character and contradictions within two large Buddhist bodies.

One especially active Buddhist movement which was nationalistic was the Lotus Sutra faith, which traditionally had developed a theory of state and a critique of politics in its own doctrine.

---

[1] *Hotoku*, a popular agrarian teaching emphasizing hard work and mutual aid.

Tanaka Chigaku (1861–1939), a former Buddhist priest of the Nichiren sect, who developed a Lotus Sutra association and criticized the sect, in 1902 completed his work *Honke Myōshu Shikimoku* and systematized a distinctive interpretation of Nichiren Buddhism. The teaching of this sect depends on the principle of *shōretsugi*[2] and was a modern Nichirenism founded on emperor worship and nationalism according to the thought of Nichiren. It considered the Meiji Constitution as the ideal manifestation of Nichiren's teaching of unity of government and Buddhism (*ōbutsu myōgō*). Tanaka's Nichirenism exerted an influence on such people as Takayama Chogyū (1871–1902) and Anesaki Masaharu (1873–1949). In 1914, Tanaka developed the new religion Kokuchūkai. Its thought was ardently supported by Nichiren schools, and also religious people of the Lotus Sutra faith and right-wing leaders. The separation and independence of various denominations within Buddhism were generally realized at the turn of the century, and each sect experienced to some degree the difficulties of the new modernization.

In Japanese society, traditionally religion did not directly participate in wedding rites, but Tanaka Chigaku, in imitation of the Christian wedding ceremony, began performing Buddhist-style wedding ceremonies in temples in the early Meiji years. In 1901, for the first time a wedding was performed in a Shintō shrine, in Hibiya Grand Shrine (Daijingū) of the Jingū Hosaikai. Again, as with Buddhism, Shintō learned from Christianity. By the time of the future emperor Taishō's wedding, Shintō-style weddings had become popularly accepted. Although these weddings were religious rites founded only in the present century, they came to be interpreted by the people as though they had been ancient Japanese customs.

[2] *Shōretsugi*, an interpretation of the Lotus Sutra in which the latter half of the sutra is considered superior to the first half. See p. 17n.

6. Christianity, Forerunner of the Social Movement

Within Christianity, the Twentieth Century United Effort Evangelism, which began in 1901, made a successful start and contributed to Christianity's social standing. During the Russo-Japanese War, while there was an anti-war movement led by Uchimura Kanzō and other Christians, support for the war was dominant, and Christians cooperated actively with the government, such as by sending clergy to minister to soldiers in the war zone. In the churches there were sermons stating that there was no contradiction between Christianity and the Imperial Rescript on Education, and the trend toward nationalism became conspicuous.

The influence of Christian social work and educational efforts, which had steadily grown since the 1880s, could not be disregarded by Shintō and Buddhist organizations. These organizations were still shouting slogans to "destroy heresy, manifest orthodoxy," but ironically it was the Christian social movements that were to impress upon these very groups the function of religion in a modern society.

The Salvation Army

One organization that stands out in the history of Christian social work is the Japanese Salvation Army, which was founded by Yamamuro Gumpei (1872–1940). Yamamuro was born into a farmer's family in Okayama Prefecture at a time when the Christian leadership of mid-Meiji was predominantly of *samurai* origin. Yamamuro was an evangelist of common background: it was while working as a printer in Tokyo and studying on his own that he entered Christianity. Yamamuro, starting in the

59

1890s worked under Ishii Jūji, a supervisor who managed an orphanage in Okayama, and busied himself in matters such as relief work in the 1891 Nōbi earthquake. In 1895 after the Sino-Japanese War, when 14 officers of the Salvation Army came from England to Japan and carried out their "declaration of war" ceremonies, Yamamuro traveled to Tokyo and joined the Salvation Army, becoming both an officer's candidate and caretaker of footwear. In 1896, the Japanese Salvation Army began its street campaigns.

The Salvation Army is an organization for Protestant evangelism and social work founded by William Booth in London in 1878. It grappled with the social evils which the development of capitalism produced, such as poverty, labor problems, unemployment, and prostitution; it was already producing actual results in various countries. Yamamuro was strongly critical of the state of Japanese Christianity which was becoming a religion of the intellectual class, aloof from the world. Because he wanted to try to preach the Gospel for the sake of the common people, he went so far as to study popular systems of moral education, *haiku*, and proverbs; he found the ideal form of evangelism in the blood and fire of the Salvation Army's holy war. Around the turn of the century, the Salvation Army put efforts into a campaign to liberate prostitutes. With a military band in the lead they marched into the Suzaki red-light district, and there was a violent fight in which they were attacked by gangsters employed by brothel managers. Even the populace who at first called them the "Christian Nichiren,"[1] came to sympathize with the heroic activities of the Salvation Army. In response to the worsening labor problems following the Russo-Japanese War, the Salvation Army opened the first Japanese employment office for aiding the unemployed. In 1907, General W. Booth came to Japan and had an interview with Emperor Meiji. Especially as this visit took place within a few years of the signing of the Anglo-Japanese Alliance, General Booth was warmly received by both the government and the people. The Imperial Household and financial circles pledged support of the Salvation Army, enabling it to increase its activities. Within

---

[1] The Nichiren tradition is famous for its aggressive evangelism and loud street activities.

two years, their street "society kettles" program was begun. With the intensification of social ills brought on by capitalism, the Salvation Army set a precedent by their campaigns to alleviate human suffering. As their medical facilities were made possible by grants from the Imperial Household, other Christian and Buddhist social welfare groups soon came to be regarded as government-recognized relief agencies.

Christian Socialism

Accompanying this gradual public acceptance of Christianity, in the early 1900s the Universalism of German liberal theology and Unitarianism were introduced. Unitarianism, in contrast to Christianity in general with its belief in the Trinity, believes in an abstract, individual, transcendent existence. It is an example of a modern, rational religion. In 1912, the Unitarian leaders Naruse Jinzō (1858–1919), Anesaki Masaharu, and others founded the Kiitsu (Unity) Kyōkai and promoted religious cooperation among Shintō, Buddhism, and Christianity. In contrast to the sect of Uchimura Kanzō, which was engrossed in an interior faith and yet also created the distinctively Japanese non-church movement, the Unitarians became the watershed of Christian socialism begun by such people as Abe Isoo (1865–1949). Abe was a graduate of Dōshisha and studied in the United States where he became a Christian socialist. In 1898, he formed the Society for the Study of Socialism, and three years later, together with Kōtoku Shūsui and others, he founded the Social Democratic party. The Japanese socialist movement was founded largely through the activities of Christian socialists who, like the anarchists and socialists, studied mainly in America.

After the Russo-Japanese War, the Christian socialist movement made remarkable progress. Following the dissolution of the socialist organization Heiminsha (Society of Common People), which had carried out an anti-war campagin, the Christian socialist leaders Kinoshita Naoe (1869–1937), Abe, Ishikawa Sanshirō (1876–1956), and other former Heiminsha activists launched the monthly journal *Shin Kigen* (literally, new era) in 1905. Although

Shin Kigen ceased publication with its thirteenth issue in November of the following year, it included articles by such writers as Tokutomi Roka and Tazoe Tetsuji (1875–1908) on Christian socialist theories. They emphasized that socialism was material Christianity, and Christianity spiritual socialism. In their social critique they advocated overcoming individual sins as well as social sins, and through Christian love realizing the Kingdom of God on earth. With the Taigyaku Incident, the socialist movement faced a dark period, and the movement of Christian socialism inevitably disappeared into obscurity.

Yūaikai, the First Labor Union

However, Christian socialism still did continue a quiet growth secretly. On the day when the Meiji era changed to the Taishō era, August 1, 1912, 14 laborers, led by Suzuki Bunji (1885–1946), gathered for the Unitarian's Unity Christianity Liberal Association held in the Yuiitsu Hall at Mita in Tokyo and established the Yūaikai (Friendship Association). The monthly membership dues were five *sen*. The Friendship Association was Japan's first labor union and was an organization for mutual aid and cooperation between labor and capital, named after England's friendly societies. Suzuki, while a student in Yamaguchi High School, accepted the teaching of Homma Shumpei (1873–1948), a Christian evangelist who worked for the reform of ex-convicts and earned the name of "saint of Akiyoshidai," and later entered the Unity Christianity Liberal Association. The difficult working conditions of laborers and their sense of a life with no future hope inspired Suzuki with humanism, and although his plan was humble, he worked to organize laborers. At the same time the young theological student Kagawa Toyohiko (1888–1960), who was a Christian socialist activist, settled into the Shinkawa slum district of Kobe on his own and continued his evangelism among day laborers, the unemployed, beggars, prostitutes, and habitual criminal offenders. Kagawa earned the name of "saint of the slums" and became the topic of conversation in Christian circles, but he became disillusioned with his evangelism and thus ended his career of self-sacrifice, and he went to America in 1914 for further studies. Kagawa observed the flourishing American labor movement and returned to Japan with the resolve to try to create a powerful labor union.

The Friendship Association existed within difficult political conditions and because it was an irreplaceable labor organization, whenever labor disputes arose its assistance was sought, and the association's fame was increased with every dispute favorably settled under its leadership. Two years after its founding, World War I began, and the organization of the Friendship Association expanded rapidly.

In 1914, members of the Friendship Association numbered 6,500 and at the beginning of 1916 under wartime prosperity topped 10,000 members, doubling by September of that year. The organization spread from the Tokyo area to the Kyoto-Osaka area, Kyūshū, and Hokkaidō. The character of the Friendship Association, together with the development of the labor movement, began to change from the original friendly gathering for cooperation between labor and capital, to a labor union federation. Future labor and socialist leaders Kitazawa Shinjirō, Yamamoto Kenzō, Nosaka Sanzō, Asō Hisashi, and Akamatsu Katsumaro received their training here, and the Friendship Association developed into the Sōdōmei (General Alliance).

Kagawa participated in the Friendship Association in 1916, becoming a labor leader in the Kyoto-Osaka area, and led the great strike of the Mitsubishi and Kawasaki shipyards in Kobe. After the resolution of this bloody labor dispute, Kagawa, together with Sugiyama Genjirō, set up Japan's first farmers' cooperative, at the same time gathering young evangelists and organizing the Friends of Jesus Society (Iesu no Tomo Kai), and shifting to social improvement projects, such as cooperative movements. The service of practical activities by Christian socialism in the first quarter of this century abounded with the remarkable idealism of the early social movements and is of great historical significance as the social practice of religion under the system of State Shintō.

Compared to the social advances of Protestant groups, Catholicism since the beginning of Meiji poured most of its energies into bringing back into the church the Christians who remained in Nagasaki, Sasebo, the Nishi Sonogi Peninsula, and Gotō Islands.

Their missionary activities on a nationwide scale were finally begun in earnest in 1891 under the ministry of Archbishop Osouf in Tokyo, on order of Pope Leo XIII. However, Catholicism's stronghold was still primarily in Nagasaki Prefecture, and the majority of clergy were either foreigners or from Nagasaki Prefecture. Their social work and educational institutions were founded and managed mainly by foreign Catholic orders, and the church built a small but solid following throughout the country.

As a rather feudalistic form of Christianity, the Russian Orthodox (Harisutosu) Church, which founded the Nicholai Cathedral in Tokyo in 1891, had within its nature characteristics favorable for its development within Japanese society. However, because it was of Russian origin, its activities were checked by the antiforeign sentiment and anti-Russian propaganda at the time of the Russo-Japanese War. During the Russo-Japanese War, Archbishop Nicholai took the initiative to pray for Japanese victory, also providing protection and evangelization for Russian Army prisoners.

Religious Cooperation

As officially recognized religions, Sect Shintō, Buddhism, and Christianity supported the edification of the people under the emperor system, and cooperative interchange between these religions increased. In 1906 the Religionists' Concord Association consisting of various religious leaders was created, forming the start of a religious cooperation movement.

In February of 1912, two years after the Taigyaku Incident, at the suggestion of Vice-Minister for Home Affairs Tokonami Takejirō, representatives of Sect Shintō, Buddhism, and Christianity gathered together for an assembly of the three religions. The representatives resolved to "support the Imperial Household and increasingly to plan for the promotion of national morality." The religious policy of the government charted an undisguised course of strengthening the cooperation of Sect Shintō, Buddhism, and Christianity for political advantage.

7. The Reorganization of Shrines

The Sino-Japanese and Russo-Japanese wars fanned the nationalistic and militaristic feelings of the populace, and shrines throughout the country once again became active as agencies for the propagation of State Shintō. While preserving their traditional role in local rituals, shrines poured their energies into the diffusion and propagandizing of emperor worship and nationalism. Since the promulgation of the Meiji Constitution, a movement within Shrine Shintō to restore the Department of Shintō, demanding the reinstatement of the early Shintō theocracy, was revived. In 1898, the National Association of Shintō Priests (Zenkoku Shinshokukai) was founded and planned to strengthen the privileged position of Shrine Shintō as the maintainer of state rituals, and therefore superior to Sect Shintō, Buddhism, and Christianity.

In 1899, the Ministry of Education issued a directive in which religion was to be strictly separated from educational institutions. In order to be certified as ordinary schools, the religious education of religiously affiliated schools was severely restricted. This restriction was intended to strengthen the education based on State Shintō, and dealt a heavy blow to the schools of Christian affiliation. The Public Peace and Order Police Law which was enacted in the next year, 1900, prohibited membership in political parties by Shintō, Christian, and Buddhist clergy, as well as other religious leaders. By virtue of the fact that persons with religious occupation were deprived of eligibility for election and forbidden to be active in politics, they were almost completely depoliticized, and the government created a situation in which it could take advantage of the politically powerless religionists.

Shrines Under Government Control

In 1906, after the Russo-Japanese War, full-scale merger plans for nationwide shrines were launched under the direction of Hara Takashi, the Minister for Home Affairs. There were 190,265 shrines in that year, the majority of which were small regional shrines, such as village shrines and shrines with no rank. These small shrines had no specific Shintō clergy. There were many instances where members of the village centering around the shrine rotated in serving as priests. Accompanying the consolidation of local systems at the turn of the century, the Shintō parish system was revised, making powerful local leaders the parish representatives. Not entrusting the management of shrines to the local common people, in order for state and local authorities to have complete control over them, a drastic amalgamation program affecting a large number of shrines was carried out. The number of shrines was decreased to 110,000 (of which village shrines were about 44,000, and shrines with no rank were about 60,000). Then in 1907, the Ministry of Home Affairs instituted a system of shrine ceremonies, bringing rituals, too, under uniform control.

As a result of this, in the shrines of every region in the country, the festivals which had been formed in close connection with local customs were all reorganized. These festivals were transformed into the rites of State Shintō, with both the date and form of the festivals being imposed from above. The promotion of Japanese folklore studies, centering around Yanagita Kunio, was greatly motivated by the concern for Japan's indigenous religious customs and practices which were about to perish due to shrine reorganization and government enactments concerning ritual at this time.

The other side of this "rationalization," which was advanced as the merger and reorganization of the tradition-laden shrines, is seen in the fact that the government since the Meiji Restoration founded a small number of very high ranking shrines (of *jingū* and *jinja* level).[1] Of these shrines, in terms of lineage, they can be separated into about five groups: 1) those which take as their

---

[1] *Jinja* is the usual term for Shintō shrines, while *jingū* is reserved for major shrines.

enshrined *kami* the emperor or members of the imperial family; 2) those which take as their enshrined *kami* the military commanders on the side of the southern court in the period of the Northern and Southern Dynasties;[2] 3) Yasukuni Shrine and shrines for the war dead (*shōkonsha,* later renamed "country-protecting" shrines, *gokoku jinja,* which took as their enshrined *kami* the men killed in action on the imperial side in the civil war during the Meiji Restoration and the war dead under the modern emperor system); 4) the shrines in Hokkaidō, the new territories, and colonies; 5) the shrines which took as their enshrined *kami* feudal lords of the Tokugawa period.

Almost all these shrines were granted the high rank of imperial and national shrines, and except for those which venerated former feudal lords, were built for political purposes, expending enormous state funds. Out of all of them, the shrines which took emperors and imperial family as their enshrined *kami* existed as the favorites of State Shintō. In rapid succession, first there was the founding in 1881 of Yoshino Shrine (Jingū), which took Emperor Godaigo as its enshrined *kami*; then, in the next year, there was Kashiwara Shrine (Jingū) for Emperor Jimmu, and in 1895 Heian Shrine (Jingū) for Emperor Kammu was dedicated anew. Among shrines which venerated the "loyal subjects" of the southern court, following the foundation of Minatogawa Shrine for twelfth-century military leader Kusunoki Masashige, others enshrining such historical loyalists as Nitta Yoshisada, Kusunoki Masatsura, and Kikuchi Taketoki were established. Kikuchi Shrine in Waiu, Kumamoto Prefecture, has an exceptional history in its elevation of status. It was founded by a feudal clan in 1880, and in 1883 it became a district shrine; in 1895 it became a prefectural shrine; and in 1898 it became a special imperial shrine. In 1911 the problem of the legitimacy of the southern court case was brought before the Diet, and the argument for the legitimacy of the southern court was nothing more than a fictitious argument that State Shintō had created since the beginning of Meiji.

---

[2] In the fourteenth century there were two competing imperial courts, the northern and southern. The southern court eventually abdicated to the northern court, but many warriors devoted to the cause of the imperial rule gave their lives supporting the southern court, and Shintō scholars have traditionally sided with the southern court.

The Building of Meiji Shrine

In 1912, the year that the Sect Shintō–Buddhist–Christian Religious Assembly was held, the era changed from Meiji to Taishō (1912–26). State Shintō was completed as a system with the official recognition of Tenri-kyō as an independent group in 1908. The next year, with the transfer of the Bureau of Religion from the Home Ministry to the Ministry of Education, administration of shrines came under the Home Ministry (in the Bureau of Shrines), and administration of religions came under the jurisdiction of the Ministry of Education, such that the two were completely separated.

In 1914, World War I broke out, and Japan declared war on Germany. In World War I, Japan took advantage of the temporary retreat of European imperialism during the hostilities and expanded its market, first in China and then to Southeast Asia and South America, enjoying the unprecedented war prosperity. In China, through aggressive military advances, it demanded an unequal treaty and tried to gain exclusive rights to the Chinese market. During World War I, investment in equipment rapidly expanded, and the production of both heavy and light industries was increased. Large monopolies loomed above smaller businesses and prospered as they edged them out of the market by shifting the blame for financial crises on them. Japan's dual-structured capitalism was thus created in this process of rapid growth.

Together with the development of capitalism, there was a heightening of the political and economic demands of citizens, with farmers, laborers, and salaried people forming the main force of these demands. Under the label of "Taishō democracy," there were movements for the safeguarding of the Constitution and for universal suffrage. In Buddhist and Shintō circles there was a movement demanding political participation, which succeeded in gaining eligibility for election.

The Taishō era, which experienced World War I, rice riots, postwar panic, and the devastating 1923 Tokyo earthquake, was a politically unstable period, with successive upheavals manifested in movements of the people. A modern citizens' consciousness finally took root in Japanese society, a result of this turbulent period.

In this period, Meiji Shrine (Jingū), as a religious monument of the modern emperor system, was constructed as a national people's movement. The proposal for the construction of Meiji Shrine venerating Emperor Meiji was arranged informally within the Imperial Court in 1913. It organized construction groups formed on popular loyalty and affection for the great emperor Meiji, "the wise ruler who opened up modern Japan," and construction began in 1915. For the building site Yoyogi in Tokyo was chosen, with the imperial estate of Minami Toshima as the inner garden, and the Aoyama parade grounds, which had been prepared as the formal grounds for the imperial funeral of Emperor Meiji, as the outer garden. The construction took five years and cost 5,200,000 yen in national funds. Volunteer youth groups from throughout the country participated, and the Kokuchūkai and all religious bodies of Shintō and Buddhism also contributed. Before the completion of construction, Empress Dowager Shōken died, and plans were changed so that both the emperor and empress dowager would be the enshrined *kami*. Meiji Shrine was completed in November, 1920, commemorated with a magnificent enshrinement ceremony and bestowing on it the rank of imperial shrine of major grade.

Throughout Japan's recent history we find no parallel for the construction of a huge religious institution built on such a grand scale as Meiji Shrine. Meiji Shrine was administered by four bodies— metropolitan Tokyo, the city of Tokyo, the Tokyo Chamber of Commerce and Industry, and the Meiji Shrine Support Society—as the chief representative religious institution of the Greater Japanese empire. It attracted large numbers of worshipers, especially at New Year's and on the anniversary of Emperor Meiji's birthday (formally observed since 1927). They disseminated the "sacred virtue" of Emperor Meiji, and were effective in promoting emperor worship. Furthermore, from the beginning of construction, the building of a large stadium was planned in the outer garden. This plan emerged from the notion that the nation's people— young and old, male and female—gathering before the hallowed spirit of Emperor Meiji, would show that even after his death the nation lives on harmoniously in mutual love and the state prospers.

8. The World Renewal Religions: Ōmoto-kyō and Hommichi

Tenri-kyō in the 1880s was promising "salvation of the myriads in the three thousand worlds" through its main deity Tenri-Ō-no-Mikoto and developed its propagation program to spread Tenri teachings to Japan and the world. The establishment of State Shintō meant a system of severe oppression of independent popular religious movements, and Tenri-kyō came to be viewed as a heretical religion along with Maruyama-kyō and Remmon-kyō and suffered persistent persecution, threatened with the label of *lèse majesté*. With its legalization and nationwide propagation, Tenri-kyō, a world renewal religion, diminished its anti-establishment character. During the Sino-Japanese War, it participated in the national policy in such ways as contributing 20,000 yen for shipbuilding and war armaments, and in 1903 published *Tenri-kyō Kyōten* (Tenri-kyō Scripture) in conformance with State Shintō ideology.[1] The full-scale development of capitalism saw an intensification of a demand for world renewal—a religious expression of emancipation—and new religions were to appear on the scene, religions that would not fit into the State Shintō framework.

Deguchi Nao and Ōmoto-kyō

Ōmoto-kyō was founded at Ayabe, Kyoto Prefecture, in 1892 preceding the Sino-Japanese War, and constitutes a typical world

---

[1] The original teachings of Nakayama Miki, founder of Tenri-kyō, were recorded in the simple Japanese syllabary that most people could read, but the later *Tenri-kyō Kyōten* utilized the complicated terms borrowed from Chinese that characterized more formal, "bookish" Japanese. This is another indication of Tenri-kyō's departure from the founder's initial teachings and its increasing conformity to bureaucratic control.

renewal religion under the modern emperor system. The founder of Ōmoto-kyō, Deguchi Nao (1837–1918), urged the realization of the ideal world of Miroku's[2] age and the salvation of the people in her *Ofudesaki*, in which she wrote: "the three thousand worlds shall burst into full bloom as the plum blossoms do! The age of the deity Konjin of the northeast direction has arrived."[3] The "Nao Group" in the last years of Meiji absorbed the folk religious tradition harking back to the feudal society and put together a distinctive syncretic Shintō doctrine.

Deguchi Nao was the widow of a poor carpenter who lived in the small town of Ayabe in the Fukuchiyama valley. Nao, who had served a *sake*-loving, self-indulgent husband and raised eight children, at the age of fifty-three lost her husband; thereafter she eked out a living with her wages as a ragpicker and silk spinner. Nao had already received advice during *kami* possession concerning the derangement of two of her daughters, and on the lunar New Year when she was 56, she had a vision and fell into an intense *kami* possession.

Nao was influenced by Konkō-kyō which was spreading its teachings into the region at this time, thus deepening her own unusual experiences through belief in Konjin of the northeast. However, the next year, 1893, she was confined to a room as an insane person, and it was there on the command of the *kami* that she began writing the *Ofudesaki* on the wall with a nail. Soon faith in Konjin spread among Nao's acquaintances, and about thirty people experienced the blessing of healing. Although Nao came into contact with Tenri-kyō in Kyoto, she before long became a Konkō-kyō missionary, continuing to write *Ofudesaki*; but six years after the founding of this teaching she left Konkō-kyō.

Nao taught belief in Konjin of the northeast as the *kami* who originally reconstructed and transformed the three thousand worlds; this doctrine inherited the doctrine of Konkō-kyō and Tenri-kyō, which reflected the demands of the people in a period of

[2] Miroku, or Maitreya, is the so-called future Buddha who is believed to usher in a new, ideal world.

[3] In traditional Japanese beliefs, Konjin was a malevolent deity residing in the northeast direction, causing illness and suffering. Later, however, especially in the new religion of Konkō-kyō, this belief came to be reversed, such that Konjin was a benevolent deity; belief in Konjin made it unnecessary to follow the innumerable rules for good and bad luck.

the collapse of a feudal society, as a popular religion at the end of the Tokugawa period. Nao, who as a pauper living in a small town witnessed the exploitation by silk-thread manufacturers then advancing in the mountainous areas of Kyoto Prefecture, was very critical of the influential rich. She opposed capitalism and the materialism of civilization and called for an idealist age of no war and a return to life based on agriculture. In her *Ofudesaki,* the eschatological viewpoint of world renewal, which the popular religions held in common, expressed an intense resentment toward society.

Nao's small following welcomed Ueda Kisaburō (1871–1948), a religious practitioner of the Inari faith, and together they created the Kommei Reigakkai. Ueda was the son of a poor farmer in the suburbs of Kameoka in Kyoto Prefecture. On the basis of his many religious experiences, he could heal the sick, and he learned syncretistic Shintō teachings and shamanistic practices from Nagasawa Katsutoshi (1858–1940), a spiritualist who led an Inari religious association (*kōsha*) in Shizuoka Prefecture. Ueda helped Nao, who was suffering from police oppression on account of her officially unrecognized missionary activities. By creating the Kommei Reigakkai in affiliation with the Inari religious association, they achieved a tentative legalization for this missionary work. The next year Ueda married Nao's fifth daughter Sumi and took on the Deguchi family name, later adopting the new name of Onisaburō.

Nao welcomed Deguchi Onisaburō and proceeded with the systematization of Ōmoto-kyō doctrine. The Tamba region surrounding Ayabe is an area in which the Izumo-affiliated myths originated, myths differing in tradition from those of the emperor system centered around Ise. Ōmoto-kyō received sand and sacred fire from Izumo Great Shrine (Taisha), calling this the sacred use (*goyō*) of fire and earth; they also received sacred water from Moto Ise Shrine, which is traditionally considered the ancient origin of Ise Shrine. Each one of these items religiously symbolized the legitimate right to rule the country.

In the same way that Tenri-kyō based its doctrine of salvation in its myth *Doroumi Kōki*, Ōmoto-kyō brought together its myth of the withdrawal of the nation's founders. This myth emphasized faith in the two *kami* Kunitokotachi-no-Mikoto and Susanoo-no-

Mikoto, holding that the founding *kami* who were the original rulers of Japan were driven out and confined by evil *kami*, causing chaos in the present world but that the time would arrive when a government of the *kami* by the legitimate rulers will be realized. The notion of the withdrawal of the nation's founders was a challenge to the myth that considers Amaterasu Ōmikami the divine ancestor of the imperial line and clearly denied the divine status of the current emperor and the legitimacy of his reign. It is fair to say that as long as the modern emperor system existed, it was inevitable that Ōmoto-kyō would be obliterated as a heretical religion for *lèse majesté*.

The missionary activities of Ōmoto-kyō at the turn of the century increasingly suffered from police interference and suppression, and at that point believers dwindled, and internal strife among the leaders broke out. Onisaburō left Ayabe, opposing Nao and the old leaders. In Kyoto he gained the status of a Shintō priest and became a ritualist at Kenkun Shrine, and later turned to Ontake-kyō.

In 1908 Onisaburō returned to Ayabe, a man well traveled in the religious circles of the Kyoto-Osaka area, and who had broadened his viewpoint, with plans for the expansion of Ōmoto-kyō. Onisaburō was strongly opposed to capitalists and landlords and denounced war as nothing more than profit for the government; only in these points did he hold great sympathy with the spirit of Nao's *Ofudesaki*. The Kommei Reigakkai, in the midst of police oppression, grew into the Dai Nihon Shusaikai (the Japanese Purification Society), and then the Kōdō Ōmoto (Imperial Way Great Foundation). In 1914 when World War I began, Ōmoto-kyō, finding the time ripe for a reorganization of the world, began intensive propagation campaigns in the streets of Tokyo, Kyoto, and Osaka. The destitution, social instability, and rural poverty brought about by Japanese capitalism—which had accomplished the industrial revolution and entered into the stage of imperialism—created the ideal conditions for the sudden development of Ōmoto-kyō. Various people entered Ōmoto-kyō: intellectuals, such as Asano Wasaburō (1873–1935), scholar of English literature and professor at the Naval Engine School, the medical doctor Kishi Itta, and the young literary figure Taniguchi Masaharu (1893–), who had studied at Waseda

University; there were also prominent military figures and businessmen. Kōdō Ōmoto, in accordance with the government edification policy, followed a Shintoistic doctrine that emphasized patriotism. They preached a strong eschatological viewpoint and rites of group possession (such as *saniwa* and *chinkon kishin*),[4] and numerous evangelists (*sendenshi*) actively sought converts. The "Taishō Restoration" was advocated, and it prophesied that it would take place when Ayabe became the capital of the *kami*. Asano was a leading member of the organization and supervised their periodical, *Shinreikai* (World of *Kami* Spirit), which preached its message of purification of the soul.

Onisaburō experienced the self-enlightenment that he himself was the Buddhist savior Miroku and advocated a reorganization of the world which was anti-establishmentarian in character. In 1918, Deguchi Nao died at the age of 81, and in the tradition of female succession, her daughter Sumi became the second spiritual head. In 1920, three months before the completion of Meiji Shrine, the Miroku Hall was built as the central sanctuary in Ayabe. The same year, Ōmoto-kyō purchased for 500,000 yen the influential Osaka daily newspaper, *Taishō Nichinichi Shimbun*. Ōmoto-kyō's effect on society, with its prediction of the approaching end of the world, was so great that the government could not overlook it. Established religions and journalism were highly critical of Ōmoto-kyō and labeled it a heretical religion. In 1921, the Kyoto Prefectural Police, under the direction of Hiranuma Kiichirō, the head prosecutor, raided the Ōmoto-kyō headquarters with 200 armed police; they accused the leaders of the crime of *lèse majesté* and the newspaper with violation of the law. The sanctuary was destroyed, and Nao's tomb had to be reconstructed because it resembled an emperor's tomb. This First Ōmoto Incident later was dismissed in the amnesty at the time of the imperial funeral of Emperor Taishō, but Asano left Ōmoto-kyō after this incident and became absorbed in psychic research. Under Deguchi Onisaburō's leadership the organization changed its character and entered a new stage of development.

After surviving its first persecution, Ōmoto-kyō's activities expanded both within and outside the country. Onisaburō dictated

---

[4] *Saniwa* is traditionally a Shintō rite of calling *kami* to possess people. *Chinkon kishin* is traditionally a Shintō rite to pacify or purify the soul.

the large scripture *Reikai Monogatari* ("Tale of the Spirit World"), and while out on bail secretly traveled to Mongolia, where he unsuccessfully attempted to create a separate state by calling himself a living Buddha of the Lama religion. He believed that in creating a new Mongolian state and exploiting the native mounted horsemen he could help solve the problems Japan was facing, such as unemployment and food. Ōmoto-kyō responded to the promotion of the worldwide humanism and anti-war peace thought that developed following the calamities of World War I. It urged the adoption of Esperanto and the use of the Latin alphabet (for Japanese), advancing the notion that all religions have the same origin and the humanism of the brotherhood of man. It cooperated in the Chinese charitable religious organization Dōin (Tao Yuan), developing the World Religions Federated Association at Peking; within Japan it formed the Benevolence for Mankind Association (Jinrui Aizen Kai). This association spread through Asia, North and South America, and Europe, cooperating with spiritualist organizations in various countries.

These international activities which Ōmoto-kyō developed, urging world peace and love of man on the basis of a mystical conviction of the realization of a government of the *kami*, called forth considerable response overseas. Fundamentally, however, the very basis of Ōmoto-kyō while preserving an anti-authoritarian character, supported the government's imperialist expansion into Asia.

Hommichi, Sub-Sect of Tenri-kyō

Following the First Ōmoto Incident, Tenri-kyō's sub-sect Hommichi was suppressed in 1928 for the crime of *lèse majesté*. This incident came to be called the "Second Ōmoto Incident," for Hommichi, too, was a world renewal religion which challenged the religious sovereignty of the emperor. Hommichi is a religion derived from Tenri-kyō, founded in 1913 by Ōnishi Aijirō (1881–1958). Ōnishi was born to a farm family in Nara prefecture. When he was a student at the Nara Prefectural Normal School, his mother became severely ill, and he converted to Tenri-kyō. Ōnishi left school and served three years as an missionary in Gumma

Prefecture. In 1904, he returned to serve the Nara branch church of Tenri-kyō to which he had belonged, and then he was sent to another Tenri-kyō church in Yamaguchi Prefecture. Following the precedent of ardent Tenri-kyō believers, Ōnishi gathered all his assets and donated them to the headquarters before proceeding to the Yamaguchi church with his family. Ōnishi as head of the church devoted himself to the rite of *mijō tasuke* (healing the sick). From the spring of 1913, he confined himself in a room in the church and in June he fell into possession by the *kami*, attaining a self-enlightenment that he was the *kanrodai*, an inspired person, and the successor to the founder Nakayama Miki.

In Tenri-kyō, Nakayama Miki during her lifetime declared that her life span would be 115 years, but she died in 1887, 25 years earlier than she had predicted. For a while, there was the doctrinal interpretation that the following 25-year interval was considered Miki's era, and 1913 would mark the next period. However, Tenri-kyō's leaders decided that revelation ceased after the 50 years of the founder and the 20 years of Iburi Izō, the major disciple, and established a system of the religious sovereignty of the patriarch, in which the Nakayama family would retain control.

If we view the matter from the original Tenri-kyō doctrine, Tenri-Ō-no-Mikoto (who was the parent *kami*, *oyagami*), when the right time arrived, possessed Miki and bestowed a revelation; therefore it was difficult to deny the possibility that after the founder, inspired persons would appear one after another to relate new teachings. A sectarian incident in Ibaraki was followed by successive incidents within Tenri-kyō in which individuals who experienced self-enlightenment as inspired persons and considered themselves to be the legitimate successors of the founder opposed the current patriarch and headquarters. Ōnishi launched his career as an inspired person and was dismissed from the Yama-guchi church and returned to Nara Prefecture. Ōnishi secretly appealed to those within Tenri-kyō, and, amidst the panic after World War I, he established a following of farmers and merchants in the Kyoto-Osaka area. In 1924, Ōnishi was deprived of the religious rank of assistant lecturer and was expelled from Tenri-kyō. The next year he founded the Tenri Kenkyūkai (Tenri Research Association) at Takenouchi, Iwaki-mura, Nara Prefec-ture, near Osaka.

The doctrine of Hommichi taught that Ōnishi was a living *kami* identical with the *kanrodai*, and that only by his teaching (the *hommichi*, true way of the path of salvation) would Japan be saved. The *kanrodai* is a stone pillar and object of worship which was to be erected in the very center of the *jiba* as Nakayama Miki taught. The *kanrodai* receives from heaven the elixir of *kanro* (nectar or honeydew) of eternal youth and long life. Ōnishi emphasized that the true significance of the *kanrodai*, in addition to its representing earth and stone, was that it also represented human beings. Living *kami* did not cease to exist with the death of the founder, but rather, when the time came, living *kami* who possessed the principle of the *kanrodai* would appear one after another.

Hommichi developed as a powerful sub-sect of Tenri-kyō, and even on the basis of doctrinal interpretation, maintained its differences with Tenri-kyō, which was an officially recognized religion. Hommichi believed in the doctrine put forth at the time of the founding of the religion and the myth *Doroumi Kōki*. Thus, it advanced in the direction of what should be called original or primitive Tenri-kyō, and severely cricitized Tenri-kyō which had acquiesced to the emperor system. Ōnishi, by healing the sick, was actively propagating his message of warning and prophecy of the times for the realization of a government of the *kami*.

In 1927, Ōnishi considered the severe illness of his oldest son as a serious warning of the parent *kami*, and he decided to make public his previous writings on the salvation of the world and the nation. This pamphlet was called "Kenkyū Shiryō" ("research materials"); it warned that a world war would erupt and Japan would stand on the edge of destruction: only through the teaching of the living *kami* identical with the *kanrodai* could the danger be escaped. Moreover, he wrote from the same standpoint as original Tenri-kyō and denied the divine character of the emperor. He asserted that since the early writings about the age of the *kami* were fictitious, the emperor as based on these writings had no right to rule the state. The followers of Hommichi accepted the orders of Ōnishi and organized propagation teams, and from March of 1928 they distributed the "Kenkyū Shiryō" and spread its message throughout the country. Hommichi was particularly anxious that the leaders of the time receive this pamphlet to read about the perils facing the nation, and the propagation teams distributed this information to the private homes of influential leaders, government and public agencies, and the police.

The officers of the local Takada police station in Nara Prefecture were astounded by the treasonous wording in the pamphlets. They immediately prohibited any news on the matter and investigated Ōnishi and 500 leaders and followers throughout the country. After this, 180 persons were accused of the crime of *lèse majesté*, and the Home Ministry ordered the dissolution of the Tenri Kenkyūkai. With the lifting of the news ban, the media, as at the time of the Ōmoto Incident, wrote scathing articles on the magical and commercial character of heretical Hommichi, and the extravagant private life of Ōnishi was sensationalized.

Under the modern emperor system, the crime of *lèse majesté*, along with peace and order legislations, such as the Peace Preservation Law, was one of the government's most effective and dreaded means of controlling thought and social activities. The crime of *lèse majesté* was covered in a law created to control speech and treasonous conduct toward the emperor, the imperial household, and shrines. In actuality, guilt was decided subjectively by a judge, and as a general rule the court was held behind closed doors. Inconceivable as it may seem, as long as the emperor remained a manifest *kami* and the central expression of religion, then criticism of the emperor's shrines was punishable by the law and was a religious taboo.

However, when the Hommichi *lèse majesté* incident was brought to court, it became clear that it posed difficult problems. In the Ōmoto Incident, the situation was ambiguous because in Ōmoto-kyō's attitude toward the emperor there was a dual structure in its principle of imperial rule. Deguchi Onisaburō endlessly repeated his claim that reverence toward the imperial household would improperly place the imperial household above ordinary people, and he did not support this notion of reverence at all. The court in deliberating on the statement of Ōmoto-kyō at least was able to reach a decision. In contrast to this, in the case of Hommichi which publicly declared its denial of the divine character of the emperor, it was impossible to present an argument in the name of the emperor. There was the danger that the claim of the emperor as a manifest *kami* would be treated on the same level as the claim that Ōnishi was a living *kami*. The fact that Ōnishi's claim was concluded to be nonsense, on the contrary, meant that the rational and objective basis of the emperor's transcendent religious authority could not be questioned. The court ordered a thorough mental examination of Ōnishi, and in 1930 the Supreme Court handed down the decision that Ōnishi was not guilty. The government, in declaring Ōnishi mentally abnormal, actually evaded the issue.

9

10

11

1. A drawing showing sutras being burned during the early Meiji persecution of Buddhism (*haibutsu kishaku*). During this anti-Buddhist movement many temples were destroyed, statues defaced, and holy objects burned.

2. A drawing of a scene in which the Three Articles of Teaching Principles are being taught by a moral instructor to young children. These articles instilled religious and patriotic values and promoted emperor worship.

3. A drawing of a Tenri-kyō sermon showing a segregated seating arrangement for men and women.

4. A commemorative photograph taken during Salvation Army founder General William Booth's visit to Japan in 1907.

5. Meiji Jingū, the shrine built by volunteers from throughout the country to venerate Emperor Meiji. Photograph taken before World War II.

6. An overseas shrine, one of many built by the Japanese in their colonies throughout East and Southeast Asia.

7. Ōmoto-kyō's Gekkyūden before and after destruction (1936) carried out under the government's repression policy. On the left, Deguchi Onisaburō stands before the temple.

8. Nihonzan Myōhōji followers opposing the expansion of a U.S. air base confront riot police at Sunagawa (1955). Courtesy of Nihonzan Myōhōji.

9. Kitamura Sayo, founder of Tenshō Kōtai Jingū-kyō. Courtesy of Tenshō Kōtai Jingū-kyō.

10. Participants at the First World Conference on Religion and Peace held in Kyoto, 1970. First row, left, President Niwano Nikkyō of Risshō Kōseikai. Courtesy of World Conference on Religion and Peace.

11. Shakaden (Buddha Hall) at Reiyūkai's headquarters in Minato-ku, Tokyo. Courtesy of Reiyūkai.

III. Religious Oppression Under Militarism

1920s-1945

9. The Popularity of New Religions

After World War I, Japanese capitalism of the 1920s experienced a serious panic. The prosperity it enjoyed during the war turned into a worldwide postwar panic, and industries that had once reaped profit fell into depression. The lives of laborers, salaried men, and farmers became increasingly difficult with the rising prices, and following nationwide rice riots, there was a series of large-scale factory strikes and tenant uprisings. In 1923, an earthquake devastated Tokyo, the center of Japan's politics, economics, and the military. The people called the Tokyo earthquake a divine punishment, and out of the enormous calamity panic arose. This was a period of economic distress and social instability; the labor and farm movements developed, and the government's oppression of such movements intensified as well. Immediately after the earthquake, the "Imperial Edict for Promotion of the National Spirit" was published, and the next year the government invited representatives of all religious organizations to the prime minister's official residence, requesting their cooperation in the proper guidance of public thought. In 1925, the demand of popular movements finally bore fruit, and the universal manhood suffrage law came into existence. However, at the same time the Public Peace Preservation Law was created explicitly for the oppression of socialist movements.

The worldwide panic of the late 1920s also affected Japan, and social instability intensified. The government, using the Peace Preservation Law as a weapon, repeatedly persecuted socialist movements. The panic threatened the livelihood of laborers, and especially in northeastern Japan the financial difficulties of farmers was severe. Beginning in the 1930s, right-wing patriotic movements and fascist movements gained power, bearing the slogans of relief for farmers and political reform. Japanese capitalism pursued a course of foreign expansion, launching a full-scale war on China. It was in this process that a fascist emperor system was formed. The instability of the times provided the conditions for the growth of religions, and many new religious movements were born at this time. With the development of capitalism during World War I, the urban lower class expanded, and added to the existing middle- and lower-class farmers, the new lower middle class and the owners of small businesses became the core of supporters of religious movements. This was the initial development of the new religions, when their following began to shift from a rural to an urban base. The new religions of this period, according to the 1924 survey of the Ministry of Education, totaled 98 organizations—65 Shintō, 29 Buddhist, and 4 Christian. These organizations were distinct from Shintō and the officially recognized Buddhism and Christianity, which were granted protection and privileges. If there were some organizations not officially recognized, there were also some organizations that managed to have their missionary work legalized by becoming affiliated churches of officially recognized religions. The government called these religions semi-religious organizations (*shūkyō ruiji dantai*) or pseudo-religious organizations, (*giji shūkyō dantai*) in the sense of questionable false religions, and treated them as heretical religions. Regular religion was under the jurisdiction of the Bureau of Religion of the Ministry of Education, but these other religions came under the inspection and control of the Home Ministry. It became fashionable to indiscriminately attach the phrase "newly developed" to terms such as "newly developed housing" and "newly developed literature," and the fact that the new religions, starting from Ōmoto-kyō, were called newly developed religions was a reflection of this trend at the time.

Salvation Through New Religions

The new religions grew in size, organizing panic-stricken city dwellers and farmers, but at the same time there was an intensification of the government's thought control which aimed at the oppression of socialism. Ingratiating itself with this national policy,

Buddhism became formalized and conventionalized, and isolated itself from the daily lives of the people. Moreover, the majority of the religions of Sect Shintō became established religions, stunting their growth in the process. The people became increasingly attracted to doctrines of easy salvation directly related to their daily lives and occupations, by means of immediate, this-worldly benefits. The converts soon became devoted lay missionaries and were active in spreading the teaching. Most of the new religions attracted believers through the personal charm of a founder (*kyōso*) who held the authority of a living *kami*. There were instances where the founder and organizer were the same person, and others in which an efficient organizer joined with a founder to help direct the religion. Within the organizations the authoritarian leadership of founders and/or organizers was absolute. Professional missionaries were rare, and systems of clerical classes were undeveloped; rather, it was common for clergy and believers to be undifferentiated. The new religions derived from Buddhism were overwhelmingly lay organizations, and organizations led by priests followed a principle of equality or unity of priests and laymen.

Converts to new religions were motivated to convert by the promises of the resolution of immediate problems, such as sickness, economic distress, family discord, and personal problems. The various this-worldly benefits answered the needs of the people and gave them a new purpose in their lives. Followers believed that the *kami* and spirits were alive, that miracles actually occurred, and rejoiced in their salvation. The people's faith relied on actual proof and was satisfied by the results. Followers were indoctrinated to believe in the actual observation of *kami* and spirits and the ideological base for miracles. The group consciousness among the believers led them to a sense of missionary purpose and of elite consciousness.

The new religions that developed into nationwide organizations, without exception, incorporated the diverse and complex traditions found in Japanese religions. They actively carried out missionary work, freely relying on magical and shamanistic methods. Under the State Shintō system, Shrine Shintō only performed rituals; Buddhism's independent development was thwarted, and it was linked chiefly to its parish by funerals and memorials, in time losing its function of salvation. A capitalist society soon matured, but the established religions could only partially cope with the transformation brought on by the maturation of capitalism, and it was the new religions that assumed the role of filling this vacuum. Although they were premodern and relied on magic, they were active and dynamic religions. Despite the popular support they received, the government consistently viewed them merely as heretical religions, and the intellectual class and established religions only criticized their abnormal character as confused phenomena; they did not attempt to evaluate the social function these new religions performed. According to a Ministry of Education survey, there were 414 new religious organizations by 1930, rapidly expanding to 1,029 organizations by 1935.

Ōmoto-kyō

In the latter half of the 1920s, Tenri-kyō once again enjoyed a period of development and spread in the urban centers on a large scale. Ōmoto-kyō after its first persecution in 1921 again expanded considerably, and its international activities were also notable. Ōmoto-kyō's keynote was to support the government's expansion into Asia, strengthening its posture of serving national policy. Ōmoto-kyō's philosophy of agricultural resurgence was conceptualized and inclined toward a reform theory of a fascist state. While Ōmoto-kyō supported fascism, it also depended on an unorthodox myth challenging the emperor system. By urging both the realization of a world renewal through an age of Miroku and an international friendship through humanism, it acquired wide support of the people. Even before the first incident, Tomokiyo Yoshizane seceded from Ōmoto-kyō and founded Kakushin-kyō (later Shintō Tenkōkyo). In 1928 Kishi Itta also left Ōmoto-kyō and created Meidōkai (later Ishinkai).

Seichō no Ie

Taniguchi Masaharu, who had left Ōmoto-kyō the year after the First Ōmoto Incident, in 1929 received the revelation that "there is nothing material, only truth exists," and the next year founded Seichō no Ie in Kobe. In 1934, he went to Tokyo, where Seichō no Ie took the form of an educational foundation, and established the stock company Kōmyō Shisō Fukyūkai (Association for the

Dissemination of Bright Thought), financed by believers. Taniguchi published his own journal, *Seichō no Ie*, in which he expressed his idea of god, theory of man, and experiences of faith. Kōmyō Shisō Fukyūkai then published these under the title *Seimei no Jissō* (Truth of Life).[1]

Taniguchi explained that when we live in the "true" world as children of *kami*, sickness disappears and we are able to attain eternal life. As the foundation for this thought, he emphasized the unity of all religions and blended the diverse religious thought and philosophical concepts, especially of Shintō, Buddhism, and Christianity; he spread the rite of meditation (*shinsōkan*), which was a modern version of Ōmoto-kyō's rite of purifying the soul (*chinkon kishin*); and he also utilized psychoanalysis to explain spiritualistic phenomena. In 1935, he frequently placed large advertisements for *Seimei no Jissō* in the newspapers, and this book became a best seller. The "fellow subscribers" (believers) of Seichō no Ie exceeded 30,000, and 800,000 copies of its official magazine were published per issue. The propagation of this "bright thought" (*kōmyō shisō*), which profited from Taniguchi's publications, was welcomed by the people of small towns and the intellectual class just before World War II. While its strength as an institution increased, Seichō no Ie openly supported the government's policy of colonization and praised fascism. It preached that Japan's national polity (*kokutai*) in fact was a manifestation of the "true world" and placed emperor worship at the heart of its teachings.

Hito no Michi Kyōdan

Paralleling the major development of institutional strength of Tenri-kyō, Hito no Michi Kyōdan grew into a major force with 600,000 believers, deriving most of its strength from the Osaka area. Hito no Michi was originally Tokumitsu-kyō, founded by Kaneda Tokumitsu (1863–1919). Kaneda was a merchant of Sakai, a city near Osaka, who had deep faith in Mt. Kōya, the holy site of Shingon Buddhism and who also learned the rites of the mountain cult of Ontake and became its chief priest. In 1912, Kaneda accepted the doctrine of the Shingon esoteric tradition and became convinced both that the source of creation is Amaterasu Ōmi-

[1] Masaharu Taniguchi, *Truth of Life* (Tokyo: Seicho-no-Ie Foundation, 1961).

kami (which he considered identical to Dainichi Nyorai), the *kami* symbolized by the sun, and that man, as a spiritual particle of that *kami*, is able through asceticism to become a Buddha in this life[2] and communicate with the *kami*. Kaneda, starting out with fortune-telling for financial speculation and healing, formed the Tokumitsu Kyōkai as an affiliate of Ontake-kyō. In its doctrine, Tokumitsu-kyō accepted the ultranationalism of the Nihon Kokkyō Daidōsha, and considered the Imperial Rescript on Education its main rationale. During World War I, Tokumitsu-kyō gained a reputation among Osaka merchants and speculators. Tokumitsu-kyō formalized the folk belief of Tokugawa times that a founder could take upon himself the believers' sickness; it called this magic *ofurikae*, or "transfer."

At this time Miki Tokuharu (1871–1938) became a member of the group. Miki was the son of a merchant from Matsuyama on the island of Shikoku and became a priest of a Buddhist temple of the Ōbaku sect of Zen, but difficulties in livelihood forced him to return to secular life, and he lived for a while in poverty in Osaka. Miki was cured of a chronic illness by Kaneda, and soon after, together with his oldest son Miki Tokuchika (1900–), became a missionary for Tokumitsu-kyō. At the same time Tokumitsu-kyō spread throughout the country and was said to have 100,000 believers, but at the end of World War I Kaneda became ill and died; after the war, with the spread of economic depression, the religion dissolved. Miki and his son set up a sacred tree behind the Tokumitsu-kyō church in Osaka and were waiting for the opportunity for the revival of Tokumitsu-kyō. Then in 1924, they changed the former name of Shintō Tokumitsu-kyō to Jindō (an alternate reading for Hito no Michi) Tokumitsu-kyō.

Jindō Tokumitsu-kyō emphasized its direct descent from Tokumitsu-kyō, and a number of groups gathered around Miki Tokuharu and Tokuchika: the members of a poetry circle which Miki Tokuchika chaired, officials of Hommon Butsuryūkō, and Hashimoto Satomi (who later separated from Hito no Michi and formed the Shizensha, or Nature Society). Jindō Tokumitsu-kyō set up headquarters in Fuse near Osaka and avoided suppression by taking the Imperial Rescript on Education as its scrip-

---

[2] Become a Buddha in this life, *sokushin jōbutsu*, literally "become a Buddha in this body," a teaching emphasized in Shingon Buddhism.

ture and assuming faith in Amaterasu Ōmikami as equivalent to the Sun *Kami* (Taiyōshin), its chief *kami*. Its institutional strength expanded rapidly with its main force among the merchants and workers of Osaka, through the magical this-worldly benefits, such as the healing by *ofurikae*. In 1931, their name was changed to Hito no Michi Kyōdan. Miki used the media to disseminate his distinctively realistic morality which provided people with a simple code of conduct based on Confucian family virtue—such as harmony of husband and wife, the value of work, and dedication to place of work. After the Manchurian Incident, when fascist tendencies intensified, the practice of morning worship services flourished in Tokyo, Osaka, and in regional cities; large groups of people with badges of the rising sun on their chests gathered in the early morning at religious practice sites, and after eating a simple breakfast reverenced the *kami* and listened to a sermon.

Hito no Michi, together with Ōmoto-kyō, were both subject to severe social criticism as heretical religions because of their magical and commercial character. However, in actuality, they were only large-scale movements for edification of the people conforming to the policies of administrators.

Reiyūkai

In the latter half of the 1920s, when the promotion of nationalism flourished, faith in the Lotus Sutra, which had a long popular tradition, was also expressed in a number a new religions. Following Hommon Butsuryūkō of late Tokugawa and Remmonkyō of the Meiji era, in the Taishō era, Tanaka Chigaku's Kokuchūkai established itself, using the daily newspaper *Tengyō Mimpō* to disseminate its teaching. In 1923, the Rikken Yōseikai[3] was formed as a political body derived from Kokuchūkai and used such slogans as "purification of politics" and "unity of government and Buddhism." In 1917, Nihonzan Myōhōji, a Nichiren-derived movement, was founded with Fujii Nittatsu (1886–) as its leader.

In 1919, Reinotomo-kai (the later Reiyūkai) was formed in Tokyo as a Lotus cult by three laymen with faith in the Lotus Sutra, Kubo Kakutarō (1892–1944), Wakatsuki Chise, and Betsugi Sadao. However, this group failed, and in 1925 Kubo,

---

[3] Rikken Yōseikai, translated literally, is the Association for True Support of the Constitution.

Kotani Yasukichi (1885–1929), and Kotani's wife Kimi (1901–71) refounded the group. Kubo was an architectural technician with access to the former Imperial Household Department and was recognized by the head of the Bureau of Peerage and Heraldry. He became an adopted son of the Kubo family and was considered head of this family. His foster mother was a believer in the Lotus Sutra who occasionally became possessed. Kubo learned the faith and theory of the Lotus Sutra from Masuko Torikichi of Kokuchū-kai, and under the influence of Nishida Toshizō (1849–1918), an ascetic practitioner of the Lotus cult from Yokohama, he too became an ardent believer. While participating in the ascetic exercises of the Nakayama Hokekyō temple, Kubo came to know the spiritual talent of the shaman Wakatsuki Chise, a carpenter's wife. She, along with Betsugi Sadao, a maker of wooden combs, were the initial Reiyūkai founders.

Kotani Yasukichi was Kubo's own elder brother, a believer in the Lotus Sutra who ran a boardinghouse in the Hongo district of Tokyo. His wife Kimi was born in a poor farming family of the Miura Peninsula and as a young girl entered an apprenticeship. She married at seventeen but her husband died and later she married Kotani Yasukichi. Her own family had followed Pure Land (Jōdo) Buddhism, and only after entering the Kotani family was she taught about faith in the Lotus Sutra, but before long she came to have more ardent faith than her husband. The next year the Kotanis sold their boardinghouse and began a career as religious ascetics. Kimi's ascetic practice was first cold water ablutions and ascetic exercises to stimulate blood circulation; she frequently became possessed. In 1929, in the midst of extreme poverty, Kotani Yasukichi became ill and died, and Betsugi and Wakatsuki left Reiyūkai and founded the Shintoistic Meihōkai (the later Nihon Keishin Sūso Jishūdan).[4]

The doctrine of Reiyūkai drew upon the doctrine of Bussho Gonen (founded by Nishida Toshizō) and memorial rites for the ancestors, centering on the combination of ancestor worship and faith in the Lotus Sutra. Faith in the Buddha (equivalent to *kami*) and spirits inspired believers to have, through shamanistic and magical practices, spiritual experiences. In 1931, Kubo made a

---

[4] Nihon Keishin Sūso Jishūdan, translated literally, is the Japan Self-study Group for Devotion to the *Kami* and Veneration of Ancestors.

pilgrimage to Ise Shrine and when he was performing cold
water ablutions at dawn he gazed up at Venus, the bright morning
star (which symbolizes Kōkūzō Bosatsu).[5] Thereupon he was
enlightened by "the law of the bodhisattva that awakens Buddha
knowledge as guidance through memorial rites for the ancestors
and evangelical work," and established this as the doctrine of
Reiyūkai. Within Reiyūkai water ablutions were performed
and the rites and magic practices, such as the magical formula[6]
handed down in esoteric Buddhism and Shugendō, were held. They
made use of possession in order to demonstrate the existence of
the spirits and to heal the sick.

In the 1930s, from the Manchurian Incident to the outbreak
of war with China, Reiyūkai expanded its institutional strength
by preaching the this-worldly benefits of the Lotus Sutra and
memorial rites for the ancestors, which were based on the
family system. The name "Reiyūkai" means that the myriad
spirits of the three worlds[7] are linked with the spirit of the individual, and if one ardently memorializes one's ancestors, who are
the closest spirits, this is transformed into the memorial rites for
the myriad spirits of the three worlds. This notion means that all
men are equal. Through its premise of the salvation of individuals
and ancestors through penance and destruction of sins, it also tended to strengthen ancestor worship and patriarchal family morality,
as well as nationalism and emperor worship. In short, Reiyūkai
conformed to the time when militarism and the notions of family
and nation were prominent.

Reiyūkai's theoretical doctrine was not well developed. Rather,
it attracted believers by centering on magic and shamanism, and
providing this-worldly benefits, such as family harmony, prosperity
in business, good luck, and suppressing bad karma to heal the sick,
especially from among middle- and lower-level managers and
housewives. Ancestor worship, namely the faith in believing in the
spirits of the ancestors and trying to seek their protection to ward
off curses, is the ideological foundation of the family. Reiyūkai

---

[5] Kōkūzō Bosatsu is Ākāsa-garbha-bodhisattva in Sanskrit, the bodhisattva of space.
[6] Magical formula, *kuji*, a combination of words and gestures used to ward off evil.
[7] Spirits, *rei*, is the same as *rei* in Reiyūkai. A literal translation of Reiyūkai is Association of Spirit Friends. Three worlds, *sangai*, is a Buddhist term meaning the world
of the unenlightened.

was dependent on the Japanese family system, and it integrated the imperial state, an artificial family, with faith in the Lotus Sutra.

Resurgence of Established Religions

The fact that Ōmoto-kyō, Hommichi, and other new religions, such as Tokumitsu-kyō, Hito no Michi, Seichō no Ie, and Reiyū-kai, actively spread their teachings and within a short time developed into major religious bodies embracing large memberships clearly showed the declining influence of Sect Shintō, Buddhism, and Christianity. Through its program of edification of the people, the government impeded the penetration of socialism, and at the same time, seizing upon the public antipathy and contempt for new religions, lent its power to educational organizations which complied with the will of the government. In 1929, the Chūō Kyōka Dantai Rengōkai (Central Federation of Educational Organizations for Edification) was established, and various reactionary educational bodies of Shintō-derived ideology—such as the Kibō-sha (Hope Society) of Gotō Seikō, the Shūyō-dan (Improvement Organization) of Hasunuma Monzō (1882–), and the Hōtoku-sha (Society for the Repayment of Virtue)— increased their activities.

Also, in 1928 Hiroike Chikurō (1866–1938) left Tenri-kyō and set up the heavily Confucianist Moralogy (Dōtoku Kagaku), which was welcomed by middle- and lower-level commercial people as an ethical theory for cooperation in labor.

Within the Buddhist world, activity in social work increased in response to the intensification of social problems, and in the Shin sect of Pure Land Buddhism dissemination work in factories flourished. Also, there was a re-evaluation of Buddhism in the areas of literature and thought, especially in terms of German idealism. Within every sect of Buddhism, criticism arose against religious organizations complacently existing within a premodern temple system dependent on the family system. A series of new movements which appeared in the Buddhist world in the late 1920s went beyond the framework of organized religion and became widespread. In 1926, criticism from the Marxist viewpoint was directed against Buddhism's feudal character, its subservience to authority, and its reactionary function within society. In response to this, a counter-argument was developed in defense of religion, led by Buddhists. The Marxist argument against religion committed some Buddhists to serious self-criticism, and a movement advocating Buddhist socialism appeared. People, such as Senō Girō (1889–1961) who was called "Today's Nichiren," who were believers in the Lotus Sutra trained in Honda Nisshō's (1867–1931) "Unity Cabinet" and had led tenant uprisings, formed the Shinkō Bukkyō Seinen Dōmei (Newly Arisen Buddhist Youth Alliance) in 1931, the year when the Manchurian Incident broke out. They raised the slogans of liquidation of established Buddhism, opposition to capitalism, and establishment of a communal society. They also cooperated with socialist movements, but government suppression caused them to cease activities.

In 1932, the May 15th Incident occurred, and fascism gained power. The Ketsumeidan (Blood Brotherhood), which triggered the incident through its earlier acts of terrorism, was led by Inoue Nisshō (1886–1967), a Nichiren follower who had been influenced by Kokuchūkai. Paralleling the ominous advance of fascism, strong oppression of socialist movements continued, and Japanese imperialism's aggression in China rapidly expanded. The sense of crisis and anxiety of the times caused people of all classes, including intellectuals, to be drawn to religion. Taking advantage of this tendency, the "resurgence of religion" was advocated, and interest in religion heightened within a gloomy society dominated by fascism. This resurgence was advocated by the established religions themselves, which was confronted with both a socialist movement incompatible with national polity and the alarmingly popular new religions.

In February 1934, Tomomatsu Entai (1895–1973), who as a Buddhist intellectual had been advocating the reform of temple finances, gave a radio broadcast entitled "Lecture on the *Dhammapada* (*Hokku-kyō*)," and began the Zen Nihon Shinri Undō (All-Japan Truth Movement), with himself as its leader. This movement preached the perfection of an ideal human character according to Buddhism and called forth a great response, spreading in factories and companies.

Within Christian circles, Protestant institutional strength since the Taishō era strengthened its base among the urban middle class and intellectual class, and in line with modernization, expanded its influence in the area of literature and education. In the 1910s and early 1920s, belief in the Second Coming of Christ spread in Uchimura Kanzō's group and the Anglican Church, inspiring the establishment of Holiness organizations. The YMCA, the Salvation Army, and other groups created various kinds of facilities in the 1920s as countermeasures to such social problems as unemployment and labor problems. Leaders in the labor movement and farmers' movement who stood within reform-minded Christian socialism were active. In 1929, the Kingdom of God Movement (Kami no Kuni Undō) began, based on the reformist social creed of the Christian Federation of Japan (Nihon Kirisuto-kyō Remmei), with Kagawa Toyohiko as its leader. In five years of propagation it produced considerable results and attracted international attention. About this time the crisis theology of K. Barth and E. Brunner was transmitted to Japan from Europe and exerted a great influence by stimulating questions of faith and social practice. Nakajima Shigeru (1888–1946) and others created the Social-Christian Alliance and encouraged the social practice of Christianity. In 1930, the Student Christian Movement[8] was established and published its journal *Kaitakusha* (Pioneer), around the time the Newly Arisen Buddhist Youth Alliance was founded. The Student Christian Movement opposed social democracy and cooperated with socialist movements, but due to suppression its activity was curbed.

The Antireligion Movement

In 1926, the first year of Shōwa—in the midst of the strengthening of thought control, the growth of new religions, and the vitalization of social work both within and outside the bodies of the established religions—an antireligion movement began in Japan as a part of as the international atheist movement. The antireligion movement formed one aspect of the proletarian

[8] The Student Christian Movement is an international movement founded in European and North American countries in the nineteenth century and is especially known for its missionary activities.

cultural movement. It was based on the Marxist scientific world view which interpreted the function of religion as reactionary. In 1931, Akita Ujaku (1883–1962), Kawauchi Tadahiko, Sano Kesami (1886–1945), and others formed the Alliance for Anti-religion Combat (Han-Shūkyō Tōsō Dōmei), later to become the Japan Militant Atheists Alliance (Nihon Sentōteki Mushinronsha Dōmei). Separate from this group, Sakai Toshihiko (1870–1933), Takatsu Seidō (1893–1974), and others formed the Japan Antireligion Alliance (Nihon Han-Shūkyō Dōmei) affiliated with social democracy. The Antireligion Combat Alliance advocated opposition to imperialistic wars, opposition to preaching in factories, freedom for laborers and farmers to use religious facilities for their meetings, rejection of fund-raising, and the overthrow of reactionary educational organizations. The Antireligion Alliance was mainly an edification movement which called for the overthrow of all forms of religion. The antireligion movement mainly attacked Buddhism, Japan's largest religious force, but its greatest objective was none other than an ideological critique of the religious authority of the emperor system as based on myth. The antireligion movement was harshly oppressed and after three years it folded. However, this systematic and ethical critique, which was developed in defiance of the trend of "resurgence of religion," exerted a major impact and stimulus on every religion.

10. Persecution Under the Emperor System

Under successive oppression under the Peace Preservation Law, organized revolutionary cultural and social movements had no alternative but to retreat. Thought control under the Peace Preservation Law in 1928 was extremely severe. Organizers of societies which repudiated private property and plotted against the national policy were subject to harsh penalties, including the death penalty. As the revolutionary movements subsided, the revised Peace Preservation Law became a tool for the oppression of religion. The government invested a large amount of time and energy in observing those religious organizations which either held or potentially held heretical doctrines, in the light of the emperor system, and carried out thorough investigations and suppression. The new religions, which established themselves apart from the State Shintō system and were treated as heresies by society, were the first victims of oppression, and the government justified its control over religion by claiming the legality and authority of the emperor system.

A series of incidents—the second suppression of Ōmoto-kyō in 1935, the suppression of Hito no Michi the following year, and the second suppression of Hommichi in 1938—each of which had as its pretext either the violation of the Peace Preservation Law or *lèse majesté*, were maneuvers for the eradication of these religions. The government's suppression policy forced religious groups into currying favor with the authorities. In 1940, the Religious Organizations (Shūkyō Dantai) Law, which had as its objective the control of religion and mobilization of religion for the war effort, was enacted.

There is hardly a precedent in modern history for this set of circumstances, whereby a constitutional government, while granting freedom of religion in its Constitution, sought to eradicate specific religions, requiring their dissolution and enforcing their destruction as barbarian institutions. The extreme hatred which the bureaucracy of the emperor system showed toward these new religions brings to mind the contempt that orthodox religions have always held for heretical religions and their adherents.

Treasonous Activities of Ōmoto-kyō and Deguchi Onisaburō

Ōmoto-kyō formed the Shōwa Sanctity Society (Shōwa Shinseikai) in 1934, and under its leader Deguchi Onisaburō it proceeded to the practical implementation of political reform. Taking as advisers right-wing politicians, such as Tōyama Mitsuru and Uchida Ryōhei, they urged reconstruction of a state with emphasis on the rescue of farm villages, giving first priority to agriculture. This strengthened the character of the movement as heretical fascism from below. Such political stands of Ōmoto-kyō as denunciation of the theory of the emperor as an organ of the state, and the petitioning for abolition of parliamentary government and dissolution of political parties were alarming to the government, which was simultaneously confronted by a series of *coup d'état* plots by rightists and young army officers. Deguchi was a charismatic figure who had the power to manipulate his nationwide network and its substantial resources at will, and the government could no longer tolerate the treasonous conduct of his organization.

The Kyoto Metropolitan Police Department, which in early 1935 had received a secret order to destroy Ōmoto-kyō, made its preparations for suppression in strict secrecy. Deguchi Onisaburō in early winter of that year had been solicited for financial support by the imperialistic Kōdō-ha faction of rightists and young officers in their plans for a *coup d'état*. Shortly thereafter, on December 8, a 550-man unit of armed special police made a surprise attack on Ōmoto-kyō's headquarters at Kameoka and Ayabe, arresting 210 administrators. Also, a nationwide search was conducted by the commander of the Ministry of Home Affairs Police Bureau. Deguchi Onisaburō and his wife were arrested at the Matsue church. Following the February 26th Incident in 1936, the cabinet ministers of the army and navy were required to be serving officers of the military forces, and this was a decisive step in the dominance of fascism in Japanese politics.

The same year, 62 officials of Ōmoto-kyō were indicted for the crime of *lèse majesté* and for violation of the Peace Preservation Law; the Ministry of Home Affairs immediately proscribed Ōmoto-kyō. The main point in their indictment was that they formed a society for the purpose of revolution of the national polity and plotted to seize political power, but this was a false charge which twisted the meaning of Ōmoto-kyō's Grand Festival of Miroku, which had been held March 3, 1928.

The government ordered the destruction of Ōmoto-kyō facilities without waiting for a trial. The authorities used civil engineers to destroy the imposing sanctuary and buildings, and fearing that the lumber would be used for rebuilding, they broke each piece into one-foot lengths. The concrete structure Gekkyū-den (Shrine) was dynamited; the stone statues of Jizō, Kannon, and other deities within the headquarters had their faces marred and heads cut off. The headquarters in Kameoka was reduced to rubble. In Ayabe, the birthplace of the religion, they cut down the sacred trees in the sacred garden and scraped off the engraving on the believers' tombstones indicating their rank in the religion. They even went so far as to destroy the distinctive crest of Ōmoto-kyō on wash basins. The sacred lands in both Kameoka and Ayabe were sold off at 7 *sen* per *tsubo*, and yet Ōmoto-kyō was obliged to undertake the entire cost of demolition.

The government boasted that it had obliterated Ōmoto-kyō from the face of the earth. The reason for this suppression was the authorities' fear of the infiltration of the anti-establishmentarian tradition of popular religion which was an undercurrent in Ōmoto-kyō developments—namely, the demand for reform of the government and relief to the people. In order to protect the dignity of the emperor system's authority, which was based on irrational myths, it could not tolerate the existence of Ōmoto-kyō which was based on a different myth.

While in prison, the Deguchis were subjected to torture, and although others went insane and died in prison, they insisted that the grounds for their indictment were false, and they did not yield. In Osaka the government coerced the apostasy of the believers by making them step on an Ōmoto-kyō object of worship. Thus the use of *fumie*, a Tokugawa practice in which Christians were forced to step on a Christian symbol, such as a picture of Jesus or Mary as an act of renouncing their religion, was not unique to that period, but was reinstituted in the Shōwa era to persecute Ōmoto-kyō. After a long court battle, the year after the beginning of World War II, the Deguchis were released on bail following six years and eight months of imprisonment. Bitterly resentful of the violent oppression by the authorities, Deguchi criticized the war, and convinced of Japan's defeat, he spoke against the war and preached a faith based on peace and humanism to the believers who secretly visited him.

The Suppression of Hito no Michi

In September of 1936, the year after the outbreak of the Ōmoto Incident, the same group that carried out the raid on Ōmoto-kyō made a surprise attack on Hito no Michi. Following the Ōmoto Incident, Hito no Michi members spared no efforts to avoid suppression, supporting national policy even more ardently and emphasizing emperor worship, welcoming the will of the authorities. However, the government harbored suspicions concerning this religion with its 1,000,000 followers. Through its attack on Hito no Michi, the government also sought to take advantage of the public's antipathy for and disdain of heretical religions, and display its own honor as the personification of the true teaching of the emperor system.

Hito no Michi realized the danger of their position. Miki Tokuharu suddenly retired from active participation in the religion and Miki Tokuchika succeeded him as leader of the group. However, soon after, Miki Tokuharu was arrested on the pretext of involvement in a criminal case. In 1937, the authorities indicted officials of Hito no Michi for the crime of *lèse majesté*, for disseminating magical practices and a doctrine equating Amaterasu Ōmikami to the sun. They also ordered the disbanding of Hito no Michi. In the trial, Hito no Michi's interpretation of the Imperial Rescript on Education was found unacceptable,and it was judged *lèse majesté* to regard the divine character of Amaterasu Ōmikami as the sun. The absurd interrogation during the trial included such exchanges as: "If Amaterasu Ōmikami is the sun, then does the sun have hands?" to which the reply was "Did not Amaterasu Ōmikami with her own hands grant the sacred mirror to her grandson Ninigi-no-Mikoto?"

Of the indicted officials of this religion, the next year Miki Tokuharu died of illness while out on bail. Miki Tokuchika and others repeatedly made their defense against the unjust and false charges on the basis that there had been no act of *lesè majesté*. However, due to continuous government oppression the religion finally collapsed.

The Suppression of Pacifist Hommichi

Following the suppression of Ōmoto-kyō and Hito no Michi, in 1938 during the war with China, Hommichi was subjected to renewed suppression. Hommichi, which in the 1928 suppression was eventually ignored, in the long run was unable to safely continue its religious activities during the general war mobilization.

After the first incident, Hommichi renewed its dissemination activities and increased its institutional strength remarkably among commercial and industrial workers and speculators from Osaka, and farmers from the central and southwestern areas of Honshū and Tokyo. Ōnishi Aijirō, in a crucial period of economic depression and invasion of China, as well as the rise of fascism, once more burned with a patriotic sense of mission to warn the public. From about the time of the outbreak of the war with China, Ōnishi's wife was bedridden, and Ōnishi became aware of *shun* (the *kami's* specified time) as a revelation of the *kami*. Ōnishi ordered his believers to distribute his earlier writing "Kenkyū Shiryō" and a pamphlet with a similar message, "Shoshin" (Letters), and also such other works as "Inspiration for Warriors of Patriotism." This time aiming at distribution throughout the entire nation, several million copies were distributed door to door and also sent abroad. In 1938, Ōnishi and 373 of his missionaries and believers were imprisoned; Ōnishi and 273 of these were indicted for the crime of *lèse majesté* and the violation of the Public Peace Preservation Law, and Hommichi was proscribed. Ōnishi spent more than seven years in the Osaka and other prisons, until the end of World War II, while the case remained in court.

The myth of *Doroumi Kōki*, which supported the denial of divinity of the emperor, was the heart of Hommichi's teachings; propagation centered on magical this-worldy benefits, as in Tenri-kyō during its founding period, and pacifism based on the cooperative spirit of farm villages were upheld. Ōnishi was strongly opposed to war, and his believers were not permitted to bear arms, or even to participate in the war effort in any way. Hommichi's extreme pacifism was something that could not be tolerated by the bureaucrats charged with organizing the war effort. Without waiting for a court decision, the authorities had the Ōnishi residence in Osaka "voluntarily" vacated and forced the liquidation of the estate, with two-thirds of the estate being confiscated nominally as a donation for national defense. In the first trial, judgment was passed for Ōnishi to serve an unlimited term of imprisonment, and while the case was being appealed the war ended.

The Heterodoxy of Tenri-kyō

Tenri-kyō, which as one sect of Sect Shintō was a recognized religion, treated the Hommichi splinter group—twice suppressed—as a scapegoat and criticized its "heretical" doctrine. However, Tenri-kyō itself was under observation by a secret directive of the Ministry of Home Affairs until after the Sino-Japanese War. Even within Sect Shintō, by virtue of its popular character, Tenri-kyō, like Konkō-kyō, was secretly considered "heterodoxy" and received discriminatory treatment. The intensification of control of religion led to raising the question once more of the substance of the "*lèse majesté*" harbored by Tenri-kyō, the largest religion to arise since late Tokugawa and early Meiji.

In 1938, Tenri-kyō was advised by the Ministry of Home Affairs to revise its scriptures, because its doctrine did not contain the notion of unity with the emperor. Tenri-kyō of its own accord deleted the *Kōki* from its scriptures and established a basic policy of full support of the government and participation in the war. A large number of scriptures from the entire country were collected and turned into cardboard at a paper mill in Ōtsu,

Shiga Prefecture, in the presence of the prefectural special secret police. There was resistance to this oppression among the believers, and there were many who secretly kept their copies of scriptures. By conforming to this pressure, Tenri-kyō increasingly changed its posture to undisguised participation in the war.

The Enactment of the Religious Organizations Law

From the February 26th Incident in 1936 to the war with China and World War II, Japan became further embroiled in a ruinous war. Fascism was accompanied by intensified control and suppression of religion. In April, 1939, under the Hiranuma cabinet the Religious Organizations Law was approved, and in April of the next year it was enacted. Since mid-Meiji there had occasionally been strong attempts to enact a religious organizations law, but a strong opposition movement arose, mainly among Buddhists (for various reasons, including the fact that Buddhism would be treated in the same category as Christianity); each time the attempt failed. The government considered control of religion in line with fascism as a main pillar of its program and quickly secured approval of the pending Religious Organizations Law. As a result of the previous suppression of religions, there was little opposition to it. In his explanation of the reason for the proposal, Education Minister Araki Sadao said that the Religious Organizations Law was inevitable: religion must conform to the government which was in state of emergency and must participate in the war objectives; and to achieve this the supervision, control, protection, and nurture of all religions as a group would be more effective than for each religion to do so individually.

One extreme group within the country's leadership demanded a return to early Meiji's unification of all religions through Shintō as a state religion. However, this was a historical irony because this demand contradicted the article of freedom of religion in the Meiji Constitution. But it was agreed by the ruling class to strengthen Shintō's position, and the year when the Religious Organizations Law was enacted coincided with the ceremonies for the 2,600th anniversary of the founding of the Japanese empire, which was celebrated in November of 1940. The Bureau of Shrines within the Ministry of Home Affairs was raised in rank to the external Shrine Board within the same Ministry. For Shintō, this was a recovery of lost territory after a lapse of 70 years when the Department of Shintō was lowered in rank to Shintō Ministry, but the Shrine Board was to last only four years, ended by Japan's defeat in World War II.

Christianity Victimized

Even before the enforcement of the Religious Organizations Law, preparations for the control of religion were underway. In 1941, all religious groups were integrated under one new system of religion. Sect Shintō remained unchanged with 13 sects. For Buddhism, under the principle that groups accepting the same founder formed one denomination, the former 13 sects and 56 denominations were consolidated into 13 sects and 28 denominations. For Christianity the policy followed was to recognize two religious organizations: the Church of Christ in Japan[1] for the various Protestant groups, and the Roman Catholic Church. However, the Russian Orthodox Church and the Anglican Church did not accede to the consolidation.

The main current of Christianity followed a path of undisguised participation in the war and national policy in various ways: it formed the Tō-A Dendōkai (Association for East Asian Evangelism) in 1938 and sent military chaplains to the Chinese continent; it advocated an "imperial Christianity" (Kōdō Kirisutokyō) in harmony with Shintō during World War II. However, the general notion of Christianity as a foreign religion opposed to the Japanese polity did not weaken. Already in March, 1938, the Osaka military police published a questionnaire for churches under its jurisdiction, and through such questions as "Which do you revere, Jesus Christ or the Emperor?" attempted to create an excuse to suppress Christianity. In 1939, Akashi Junzō (1889–1965) and other members of the Japanese Watchtower (Bible and Tract) Society announced their conscientious objection to military service and were persecuted.

[1] Church of Christ in Japan, Nihon Kirisuto Kyōdan, formed in 1941 by more than 30 Protestant denominations, which were pressured by the government to unite.

In 1940 the leaders of the Salvation Army were arrested on suspicion of serving as English spies. The objective of this move was the suppression of the Salvation Army as a religion which had its headquarters in England, an enemy country. Yamamuro Gumpei's book *Heimin no Fukuon* (Gospel for Common People) was banned for a second time, as part of this measure. The government not only made the Salvation Army sever ties with England, but also required a change in their name to "Salvation Organization," for the reason that in Japan there could be no army besides the imperial army of His Majesty the Emperor. During World War II a number of churches were suppressed and victimized on the charges of the crime of *lèse majesté* and violation of the Peace Preservation Law: the Anglican Church, various churches based on adventist faith (including the Nihon Sei Kyōkai and Kiyome Kyōkai), and Seventh Day Adventist Church.

Within Roman Catholicism, already in 1919 a papal embassy was opened in Tokyo, and in 1942 during the war with China the Japanese government sent its first ambassador to the Vatican and established diplomatic relations, in spite of opposition from both Shintō and Buddhist organizations. The Vatican, which in the Lateran Treaty was guaranteed the status of a state independent of Italy, had friendly relations with fascist Italy; the Japanese government made its tie with the Vatican out of diplomatic necessity stemming from the fact that it became an Axis Power together with Germany and Italy. However, within Japan there was repeated suppression and intervention directed at the Catholic Church, a religion based on worldwide spiritual catholicism; during World War II there were incidents in Yokohama of police shooting Catholic priests to death. Within the Russian Orthodox Church the elderly Archbishop Sergei was arrested on suspicion of being a Russian spy involved in the Sorge spy incident. He was released shortly before the end of the war, but before long he died of illness, partly as a result of his severe treatment in jail. Yanaihara Tadao (1893–1961) of the Non-Church Movement because of his liberal views was driven from his post at Tokyo University, but he secretly continued his opposition to the war through his journal *Kashin* (Good Tidings).

Restrictions on Pure Land Buddhism

As the government stepped up its control of religion, religious organizations became more earnest in their participation in the war. Although Imperial Buddhism (Kōdō Bukkyō) was extolled, Pure Land Buddhism was criticized for its lack of enthusiasm in the veneration of myths. Even Nichiren Buddhism, which was ardently advocating emperor worship and nationalism, was brought to task for treating Amaterasu Ōmikami as a *banshin* (guardian *kami*) of the Lotus Sutra; inscribing the name of Amaterasu Ōmikami on the lower part of a mandala was considered disrespectful.

Nyorai-kyō, which dated from the Tokugawa period, had become an affiliate of the Sōtō Zen sect (as Nyorai-shū), but the police did not overlook even this small organization of several thousand members: the group was suppressed and its scripture *Okyōsama*, which described the founder's possession and the creation of the world, was confiscated.

The Nihonzan Myōhōji, whose teaching advocated its westward evangelization, spreading from Japan to China and India, established its institutional strength among Japanese residents in Manchuria. In its doctrine, emperor worship, nationalism, and pan-Asianism were emphasized; their leader Fujii Nittatsu gave assistance to Gandhi's anti-British independence movement in India.

Seichō no Ie's Kōmyō Shisō Fukyūkai in Manchuria actively participated in the war. Taniguchi Masaharu preached that "wherever the imperial army advances, the purpose of the *kami* is realized," and made successful propaganda campaigns among the working class in industries. During the war, due to the government's coercive thought control and Shintoistic indoctrination of the people, almost all new religions had their scope of activities curtailed, and their institutional strength stagnated. It was only Seichō no Ie that expanded its influence by its active dissemination of glorification of the war and of its emperor-centered cause.

Okada Mokichi (1882–1955), who had been head of the Ōmori branch of Ōmoto-kyō and had left the organization before the Second Ōmoto Incident, in 1934 created the Dai Nihon Kannon-kai (Greater Japan Kannon Association) which centered around

Okada's method of spiritual finger-pressure (*shiatsu*) treatment. He acquired a following by healing the sick through the power of Kannon residing within him and by using his spiritual experiences during the war for warding off bullets and for faith-healing through spiritual power emanating from his palm. However, on two occasions, in 1936 and 1940, he was arrested by the special police for doctrinal reasons and for violation of the Medical Practitioners Law. Toward the end of World War II he gained such influential believers as politicians, high military figures, and novelists. In anticipation of the end of the war, he obtained land and buildings in Hakone and Atami, and made preparations for the postwar years.

Reiyūkai and Risshō Kōseikai

Reiyūkai, a new religion of lay Nichiren origin, like Seichō no Ie, managed an extraordinary growth under wartime regulations. Reiyūkai, sensing the danger of the successive oppression of new religions, emphasized emperor worship. In 1936, they invited as their leader Kujō Nichijō of the important Nichiren temple Zuiryūji, and a member of the Sengoku tradition in which Kubo Kakutarō's foster mother had been raised. Nichijō was commonly called Murakumo Nikō, and at that time she had been expelled from the Nichiren sect due to her personal conduct, but because of her connections with the Imperial Household, she was able to avoid suppression and was thus considered the ideal leader. Kubo Kakutarō died of illness; his successor Kotani Kimi preached the defense of the home front to Reiyūkai's women. As the war situation deteriorated and people prepared for air raids by evacuating the cities, the missionary activities moved along with the evacuees and spread the teachings of Reiyūkai to the farm villages of eastern Japan, attracting as believers the professional and semi-professional religionists who worked with magic and shamanism.

Reiyūkai from its outset developed its strength on the basis of rites and religious guidance, rather than on doctrine. Branches, called vassals, *mihatagumi*, formed around spiritual leaders who were highly influential within their own branches and own believers. At the time of Kubo's death, there was opposition to

Kotani's leadership and an internal dispute intensified with powerful branches successively becoming independent. Already in 1935, Okano Shōdō (1900–79) had left Reiyūkai and founded Kōdō Kyōdan in Yokohama. Okano was originally a Tendai priest who opened a radio store in Yokohama. At the urging of Ido Seikō he joined Reiyūkai. Lotus practitioners (*gyōja*) of diverse traditions were active in Yokohama at the time, and it is said that the authorities who sought a means of controlling these activities suggested the formation of a religious organization to Okano, and he established Kōdō Kyōdan. Later Kōdō Kydaōn became a lay organization affiliated to Tendai Buddhism.

In 1938 the Dainihon Risshō Kōseikai (later Risshō Kōseikai) and Ido Seikō's Shishinkai separated from Reiyūkai. Risshō Kōseikai was established by the founder Naganuma Myōkō (1889–1957) and her organizer Niwano Nikkyō (1906–). Naganuma was born in a farm family of Saitama Prefecture and became a believer in Tenri-kyō while in her teens. Around the turn of the century, she went to Tokyo to work as a live-in servant and later became an employee in the army gunpowder works, but illness forced her to leave her work and return home. Naganuma soon was married but then divorced, and went to Tokyo a second time and remarried, opening an ice and baked sweet potato shop at Hatagaya, Shibuya. Her livelihood was assured, but Naganuma suffered from a chronic illness, and through the guidance of Niwano Nikkyō, a local milkman, she became a believer in Reiyūkai. Recovered from her illness, Naganuma studied the theories of the Lotus Sutra and rites of possession. Together with Niwano, she made daily evangelist rounds, and expanded her branch of Reiyūkai with amazing speed. Disagreements with Kotani caused Niwano and Naganuma to leave Reiyūkai and accept the guidance of Murayama Keizō, a member of Kokuchūkai. Then Niwano and Naganuma formed the Dainihon Risshō Kōseikai. The name Risshō Kōseikai is an abbreviated form of several Buddhist notions. Risshō means to stand or be established (*ritsu*) on the righteous law (*shōbō*); Kōsei means to associate (*kō*) with man while maturing (*jōju*) the Buddha body.[2]

Risshō Kōseikai adopted Reiyūkai's practices of memorial

---

[2] A complete rendering might be Association for Maintaining the Righteous Law in the Human World and Achieving Buddhahood.

rites for ancestors and the Lotus faith of destroying sins through penitence, and disseminated them along with belief in various divinities, such as Fudō, Konjin, malevolent deities (*kōjin*), and the seven gods of the body (*shichishin*), and the various beliefs and magic that Niwano had learned during his youth—the *kuji* formula, calendrical omens, onomancy, and divination. Risshō Kōseikai entered its developmental stage just before World War II, and in 1942 erected its headquarters at Wada Honchō, Suginami, in Tokyo; at that time there were more than 3,000 believers.

The Founding of Sōka Gakkai

According to the Religious Organizations Law, the various denominations of the Nichiren tradition were advised to unify under the Nichiren sect (the so-called Minobu denomination of Nichiren sect), but there was a movement to oppose this order in the Nichiren Shōshū, a group which had as its founder Nikkō, a leading disciple of Nichiren. In terms of doctrine, Nichiren Shōshū rejected all other religions as heresies, and on the basis of its interpretation of the Lotus Sutra viewed the mainstream of Nichiren sects as completely different. The main force of this opposition to unification was Sōka Kyōiku Gakkai (later Sōka Gakkai), a new religion which took the form of a laymen's organization of Nichiren Shōshū. The leader of Sōka Kyōiku Gakkai, Makiguchi Tsunesaburō (1871–1944), was an educator who had long been the principal of an elementary school in Tokyo and developed a distinctive educational theory of pragmatism called "value creation."[3] In 1930, together with the enterprising Toda Jōsei (1900–58), a junior faculty member from his school, he formed the Sōka Kyōiku Gakkai as a study group mainly for elementary school teachers. The formal inauguration of this movement was in 1937 in Tokyo, and they put their major effort into religious activities following the inauguration. Makiguchi and Toda combined the doctrine of Nichiren Shōshū and Makiguchi's book of citizen philosophy called *Kachiron*,[4] and actively disseminated this teach-

---

[3] "Value creation," *sōka*. His theory, whose complete title is *sōka kyōikugaku*, literally "value creation pedagogy," was the basis for the group's name.

[4] *Philosophy of Value* (Tokyo: Seikyo Press, 1964).

ing. Through aggressive proselytism[5] they organized elementary school faculty, shop owners, and salaried workers into discussion groups for "life renewal" with practical results; they studied the concepts of benefit and punishment in the Lotus Sutra, and the theory of value with its emphasis on beauty, gain, and the good. And they were told of the actual evidence (magical this-worldly benefits) gained from the objects of worship of Daigohonzon (a mandala in Nichiren Shōshū's head temple Taiseki-ji, near Mount Fuji).

Within the Nichiren Shōshū, forces supporting the unification with the Minobu sect, including the chief abbot and head of evangelism, were dominant. However, Sōka Kyōiku Gakkai opposed this compromise and emphasized the strict adherence to their doctrine. The government, in its efforts to control religion, ordered all religions to venerate the paper talisman of Ise Shrine, but Sōka Kyōiku Gakkai refused. In the Nichiren Shōshū doctrine, as long as the righteous law (shōbō) is not being observed, the various kami retreat to heaven and even Ise Shrine is nothing but a den of goblins; accepting the Ise talisman would therefore be slanderous of the Lotus Sutra.

By 1943, during World War II, Sōka Kyōiku Gakkai had grown to embrace 3,000 households of believers,[6] mainly in northern Kyūshū and the Tokyo-Yokohama area. Among these members there was anxiety about the aggravation of the war situation, and there was even a plan to "admonish the nation," asserting that if the nation adopted the "righteous law" it would be victorious. In the same year, Sōka Kyōiku Gakkai was suppressed on the grounds of violating the Public Peace Preservation Law and lèse majesté with regard to Shintō shrines. Sōka Kyōiku Gakkai preached

---

[5] Aggressive proselytism, shakubuku; a Buddhist term meaning to preach the teaching of the Buddha and aggressively defeat evil. Shakubuku is the opposite of shōju, persuasive means of leading people to salvation. The term shakubuku is literally break (shaku) and subdue (fuku); in the practice of Sōka Gakkai during the 1950s it was an aggressive conversion tactic in which the potential convert was subjected to persistent repetition of Sōka Gakkai's total answer to life, often in the context of group pressure, until the person converted. Sōka Gakkai has defended shakubuku as a proper method for bringing obstinate people to grateful appreciation of an absolute truth, defining shakubuku as "to propagate the True Buddhism for the happiness of other people," but the detractors of Sōka Gakkai have criticized the tactic as "browbeating" or "forced conversion."

[6] In Japan, membership in religion has often been considered in terms of households, and Sōka Gakkai (even in the postwar period) has always used this means of calculating membership.

that if the emperor converted to the Lotus Sutra, the ideal world of the unity of government and Buddhism would be realized. The organization supported the war, but nevertheless it was suppressed because of its heresy in deviating from the framework of the State Shintō system. Of the 21 administrators arrested, all renounced their faith except for Makiguchi, chairman of the board Toda, and Yajima Shūhei. Makiguchi died in prison in 1944, Toda and Yajima were found guilty, and Toda was released on bail just before the end of the war.

This period of ruthless oppression by the government from the time of war with China through World War II was a very dark one for both old and new religions. When the Religious Organizations Law was presented to the Diet, Prime Minister Hiranuma Kiichirō's statement before the Diet, "In our country the way of the *kami* (Shintō) is the absolute way, and the people of the nation all must respectfully follow it. Teachings which differ from this and conflict with it are not allowed to exist" was no mere threat; for five years thereafter it was enforced boldly with the authority of the state.

11. Shintō in the Imperial War

The Pacific War, which started in 1941 with the surprise attack on Pearl Harbor, was the consequence of Japan's course of imperialistic aggression in this century. The five-year-old war in China had fallen into a quagmire, and Japan, in order to break this deadlock, made an alliance with Nazi Germany and fascist Italy, the European countries of regressive absolutism. The alliance sought to reorganize and redistribute its influence in the world and waged an all-out war. For such a policy of aggression, State Shintō was an indispensable ideological support. In the teaching of State Shintō, the emperor was considered to be the world's only living *kami*, called the "divine emperor" (*akitsu mi kami*) or "kami in human form" (*arahitogami*). The ancestors of the emperor were called the imperial founders of the Imperial Household, and in both the preface of the Meiji Constitution and in the Rescript on Education this terminology was used. The "imperial ancestors," such as Emperor Jimmu and subsequent generations of emperors, at least were considered to be historically existing persons; but the "imperial founders" indicated the various *kami* prior to human emperors. This lineage of *kami* was traced back to Amaterasu Ōmikami, and this supreme *kami* of the myth of the emperor system granted a divine mirror to the imperial descendant Ninigi-no-Mikoto and handed down the divine decree that his descendants should rule the country. The emperors, who are the descendants of Amaterasu Ōmikami, rule Japan according to this divine decree, and under the system of State Shintō this myth was absolute in the foundation of the religious authority of the emperor.

Furthermore, the notion of the "eight corners of the world under one roof" (*hakkō ichiu*, "universal brotherhood") as based on the imperial decree of Emperor Jimmu, was actively propagated in order to justify the war of aggression. The notion of "eight directions" was a Chinese expression meaning the entire world, while the term "under one roof" meant the world is one family. This indicated that the Japanese people, who had been granted the emperor, were a superior people shouldered the mission of ruling the entire world; this was an anti-foreign, aggressive notion developed by Restoration Shintō.

Overseas Shrines

Since the Sino-Japanese War of 1894–95, through recurring wars Japan obtained Taiwan, Sakhalin, Korea, the South Sea Islands, and Manchuria as colonial or semi-colonial territories. Then from the late 1930s in the war with China and in World War II, Japan temporarily ruled the vast territory extending over the Chinese mainland, Southeast Asia, and the East Indies. According to the teachings of State Shintō, it was necessary for the Japanese *kami* to descend to those lands under Japanese rule. Almost all the overseas shrines established by State Shintō were obviously the materialization of religious aggression. Among the chief overseas shrines established prior to war with China were: 1900, Taiwan Shrine (Jinja, later Jingū); 1910, Karafuto (Sakhalin) Shrine (Jinja); 1919, Chōsen (Korea) Shrine (Jinja, later Jingū). Each of these shrines was given the designation of imperial shrine of major grade (Kampei Taisha), the highest shrine rank for a general shrine, next to Ise Shrine.

As for the enshrined *kami* at these overseas shrines, Taiwan Shrine was established to memorialize Prince Kitashirakawa-no-miya Yoshihisa who died in battle in the conquest of Taiwan, so one site was dedicated to the prince and one site was dedicated to the three *kami* noted for overseeing the country, Ōkunitama, Ōnamuchi, and Sukunahikona. Similarly, at Karafuto Shrine the same three overseeing *kami* were enshrined and were considered the pacifying agents for the northern limits of the Japanese empire and the general tutelary *kami* for the island of Karafuto. Chōsen Shrine was built in Seoul, the location of the Japanese government general of Korea, and enshrined Amaterasu Ōmikami and Emperor Meiji.

After the outbreak of war with China, an emergency order speeded up the establishment and consolidation of overseas shrines. The year 1940 marked the 2,600th year since the founding of the Japanese empire, according to traditional reckoning; in this year in the capital city Shinkyō (Hsinking or Changchun) of the Japanese puppet state of Manchukuo, as part of the religious ceremonies honoring Manchukuo, Kenkoku Shrine (Shimbyō) was established with Amaterasu Ōmikami as the enshrined *kami*. Already in the period from 1905, marking Japan's initial presence in Manchuria, until 1940, the number of shrines established in Manchuria had reached 135; among these, about 90 percent had Amaterasu Ōmikami as an enshrined kami, and about 50 percent had Emperor Meiji as an enshrined kami. At Miitsuzan (Mishan in Chinese) in the Mut'anchiang area bordering Russia and Mongolia a Hachiman Shrine was built as the northernmost Shintō shrine in Manchuria. It is said that at the time of the Nomonhan (Nomunhan) incident, Hachiman, the *kami* of war and battle, lent its divine power to the battle. The Nomonhan incident of 1939 was part of a border dispute on the frontier of Mongolia. The stunning defeat of Japan's proud and powerful Kwantung Army by Russian mechanized units was a great shock to the Japanese army. In China by 1940, 27 shrines had been established, chiefly in the areas where Japanese resided, and due to the protraction of the war with China, new shrines continued to be built.

During the war with China the following were established as imperial shrines of major grade: in Kwantung, Kantō Shrine (Jingū), with Amaterasu Ōmikami and Emperor Meiji as enshrined *kami*; in the Coral Islands, Nan'yō Shrine (Jinja), with Amaterasu Ōmikami as the enshrined *kami*. In Korea, 51 shrines were built from the time of Japan's annexation of Korea in 1910 until 1936. But during the war with China, Fuyo (Puyo) Shrine (Jingū), with the rank of imperial shrine of major grade, was established at the ancient Paekche capital of Puyo. It was to signify the "unity between Japan and Korea." The enshrined *kami* of Fuyo Shrine were the four *kami* of Emperor Ōjin, Empress Saimei, Emperor Tenji, and Empress Jingū. Thus these historical figures, who in ancient times were involved in the conquest of Korea, descended upon Korea again, this time as *kami*.

When World War II began, shrines were built in the occupied territories of the so-called Greater East Asia Co-Prosperity Sphere. Singapore was renamed Shōnantō after its occupation by the Japanese, and Shōnan Shrine (Jinja) was built. Other shrines built included San'a Shrine (Jinja) on China's Hainan Island, Akatsuki Shrine (Jinja) in Saigon, Hōkoku Shrine in Bogor (Java), and shrines were set up even in such places as Wake Island, Hong Kong, and Surabaja.

Yasukuni Jinja, the Shrine for Imperial Soldiers

Many Japanese soldiers lost their lives due to the protraction of the war and the intensification of the war. The number of war dead suddenly increased, and, as a result, the new enshrined spirits at Yasukuni Shrine (Jinja) also increased.

Yasukuni Shrine (a former *shōkonsha*) was established in 1869 at Kudan in Tokyo. At the time of its establishment it was granted extensive shrine lands with an income of 50,000 bushels of rice by Emperor Meiji as perpetual funds for ceremonies, surpassed in wealth only by Ise Shrine. In 1879 it was renamed and granted the rank of special imperial shrine (Bekkaku Kampeisha). General shrines were under the jurisdiction of the Ministry of Home Affairs, but Yasukuni Shrine alone became a special shrine under the jurisdiction of the Ministry of Army and Navy. Even in terms of its organization, Yasukuni Shrine was a religious institution of the army and navy, and generals or admirals on active duty were appointed by the emperor as organizers of special festivals. Yasukuni Shrine enshrined the war dead of the emperor's "holy wars," from the conquest of Taiwan through the Sino-Japanese War, Russo-Japanese War, World War I, the war with China, and World War II.

Yasukuni Shrine's main function was the performance of rituals for the war dead. In the late Tokugawa period, such rituals followed the tradition of consolation rites linked with belief in *goryō*, unfriendly spirits of the dead—unrelated to the funeral rites of Shintō, Confucianism, and Buddhism—in local rites for the war dead.

However, with State Shintō the ceremonies were different. Yasukuni Shrine was totally effective in implanting militarism and loyalty to the emperor among the populace since the Meiji era. "Yasukuni" means "peaceful country," but this "country" signifies the state of the imperial system. Among the soldiers who died in the civil war during the Meiji Restoration, the "rebels" (the *bakufu* troops, who fought against the new government and the emperor) were not enshrined. In other words, it was because they died for the emperor that the war dead—regardless of their conduct in life—were enshrined as *kami* and were awarded the honor of receiving the worship of the emperor, himself a *kami* in human form. Thus a soldier who died for the emperor—or state— became a *kami* and was enshrined in Yasukuni to be a spirit protecting the country and received eternal and warm consolation. This practice absorbed the traditional Japanese concept of the soul and was cleverly linked to militarism and worship of the emperor.

At Yasukuni Shrine there were two sites for the enshrined *kami*: one site for a member of the imperial family who had died in war, Prince Kitashirakawa-no-miya Nagahisa; and one site for the war dead of "subjects" numbering more than 1,200,000 by the early period of World War II. This discriminatory treatment has continued in the same fashion, even under the provisions for the Yasukuni Shrine within the present Religious Organizations Law. Yasukuni Shrine as a religious institution structurally cannot exist apart from the emperor system.

Defeat of the Land of the Kami

In 1939, the 117 regional shrines (*shōkonsha*) for the war dead throughout the country were simultaneously renamed *gokoku jinja*, "country-protecting shrines," and were in actuality to serve as local branches of Yasukuni Shrine.

From the eve of World War II, the edification of the people by Shintō intensified and *misogi*, the Shintō style of water ablutions was encouraged; the Shintō spirit of brightness, purity, and honesty was advocated. The myth of the emperor system was disseminated wholesale, and "Japan the land of the *kami*" (Shinkoku Nippon) was the government's slogan. In April, 1942, the second year of the Pacific War, in the midst of the early victories, the Religious Alliance for Asian Development (Kō-A Shūkyō Dōmei) was formed, and in November, 40 leaders of religious denominations received an audience with the emperor. The administrative scope of religion was limited, because of the government's direct control over the Shintoistic edification of the people. In the same year the Bureau of Religion was abolished and was downgraded to the Religious Affairs Section of the Ministry of Education's Bureau of Edification (later the Bureau of Educational Affairs).

The military situation in World War II reached a turning point at the Battle of Midway in June, 1942, and the Japanese troops, which had advanced throughout the South Pacific, rapidly lost their advantageous position due to the Allied counter-offensive. In 1943, Japanese troops retreated from Guadalcanal, and in March of the next year the government enforced emergency measures for a fight to the finish. In July, because of the surrender of Saipan, the Tōjō cabinet, which had imposed a dictatorial rule since the outbreak of the war, resigned. As the signs of Japan's defeat became more ominous, appeal was made to carry on the holy war; the leaders stimulated the people with the notion that in "Japan the land of the *kami,*" inevitably the *kamikaze,* divine wind, would blow. In September, the Greater Japan Religious Association for the Protection of the Country During War was created with the Minister of Education as chairman, and leaders for religious indoctrination during the war were designated. It was proclaimed that a divine land was indestructible, and an increase in the war effort was planned by investing domestic labor and materials, even to the point of having temple bells donated. However, the bombardment of Japan began in November, with the U.S. Air Force using Saipan as a base, and with material shortages and destruction from the bombardment, the country was suddenly faced with a crucial and desperate situation.

In 1945, Japanese troops retreated to Okinawa, the southern edge of Japan proper. Atomic bombs were dropped on Hiroshima and Nagasaki, and the Soviet Union entered the war against Japan. Ultimately the divine wind did not blow, and Japan, which had paid the price of 2,400,000 war dead and 750,000 civilian casualties in this war, surrendered to the Allies. "Japan the land of the *kami*" withdrew from the historical scene.

IV. The Age of Freedom of Religion

1945-1970s

12. The Separation of State and Religion

In August, 1945, the Japanese government accepted and submitted to the Potsdam Declaration which included in the tenth clause the demand for the establishment of freedom of religion. Thus after 15 years, peace returned to a land ravaged by war. The leaders of Japanese militarism expected to continue to rule the people, preserving the previous system and defending the national polity. However, the world's democratic forces, which had finally overcome the struggle against fascism, demanded the elimination of Japanese militarism. Accordingly, the Allied troops which occupied Japan proceeded rapidly with the dissolution of militarism and with democratization from above. Religion in Japan thus came to experience a great upheaval comparable to that of the Meiji Restoration.

The government had urged the people to carry out a holy war, but its expectation of divine aid was in vain, and it surrendered to the Allies. The defeat caused confusion among the people, and disorientation was widespread. During the war almost all Buddhist organizations had cooperated in the war. From the outset they were active in the domestic edification program for the war, and later became active in the missionary work among overseas troops and in the consolation of Japanese civilians living in occupied lands. However, with the defeat, not only was the Buddhist cooperation in the war completely a wasted effort, but it constituted grounds for the people to accuse Buddhism of its responsibility in the war.

The first postwar prime minister, Higashikuni-no-miya, appealed to the people for "a million-fold general repentance," and Buddhist organizations, too, repented their cooperation in the war and extolled peace, thereby staving off their loss of prestige and

118

coping with the changes brought on by democratization. One month after the defeat a Conference of Leaders of Religious Organizations was convened, and the document "Outline for Religious Edification in the Rebuilding of Japan" was published.

Freedom of Religion in the New Constitution

In October the Occupation Forces issued a directive ordering the government to remove restrictions on civil rights and freedom of religion, thus guaranteeing freedom of religion. Then in December they issued a memorandum (later referred to as the Shintō Directive) to the Japanese government entitled "Abolition of Governmental Sponsorship, Support, Perpetuation, Control, and Dissemination of State and Shrine Shintō." In addition to prohibiting State Shintō, the Occupation forces suggested that after the elements of militarism and ultranationalism were removed from Shrine Shintō, it might continue to exist as a religion without direct connection to the state.

Two weeks after the Shintō Directive, the Peace Preservation Law as well as the Religious Organizations Law were abolished; in place of the latter the government, with imperial sanction, announced the Religious Corporation Ordinance (Shūkyō Hōjin Rei). This ordinance determined that a religious group could become a corporation by registering with the government. This was a volte-face from the Religious Organizations Law whose purpose was control of religion.

On New Year's Day, 1946, Emperor Hirohito made his so-called declaration of humanity in which he denied his own divinity in the expression that the myth of the emperor system was a "fanciful notion." The emperor system and State Shintō, the absolute authority of which dominated the history of modern Japan, was simply dismissed with this declaration. The shrines lost their national and official statuses, but in 1946 the majority of shrines throughout the country organized the Association of Shintō Shrines (Jinja Honchō) as a private religious organization, with Ise Shrine as its headquarters. The other shrines continued to exist as independent religions. Following the Shintō Directive, in 1947 the Far Eastern Commission of the Occupation Forces announced its

"Basic Policy for Post-Surrender Japan." In the document it was stated: "We hereby declare the freedom of worship as well as the freedom protecting all religions, and this must be guaranteed for the future. At the same time, it must be made clear to the Japanese people that extreme nationalistic militarism and anti-democratic organizations and movements hiding under the disguise of religion will not be permitted."

On May 3, 1947, the new postwar Constitution, which specified the sovereignty of the people and renunciation of war, became effective. The twentieth article of this Constitution determined that "freedom of religion is guaranteed to all. No religious organization shall receive any privileges from the State nor exercise any political authority. No person shall be compelled to take part in any religious acts, celebration, rite or practice. The State and its organs shall refrain from religious education or any other religious activity." The eighty-ninth article specified that "no public money and other property shall be expended or appropriated for the use, benefit, or maintenance of any religious institution or association, or for any charitable, educational or benevolent enterprises not under the control of public authority."

These articles guaranteed freedom of religion as basic rights of the people in express provisions. As security for this, the separation of government and religion was specified. From the side of the people, it meant that religious belief was a private matter entrusted to the conscience of individuals; from the side of political authority, it declared its own non-religious character. Because religious belief and religious activities based thereon are private rights in the full sense, they were not granted any privileges; and state and public authority are allowed neither to protect, favor, nor support religion, nor to manage, control, supervise, or lead religion. On account of this, legal regulations concerning religion proper cannot exist in principle, and the fact that among religious groups it is possible to achieve legal status made it possible to become a religious juridical person as a non-profit corporation.

The separation of religion and government is the principle whereby state and public authority do not possess a special relationship either with a specific religion or with religion generally. If political authority supports a specific religion, then the rights of people who believe in other religions are violated, and if political authority supports religion generally, then the rights of people with no religious belief or with no religious affiliation are violated. Separation of religion and government is an indispensable prerequisite if believing and not believing in religion is to be established as a fundamental freedom. It is noteworthy that in Japan, where for more than 70 years State Shintō was forced upon the people, and where suppression of religion was successively repeated, historically no single religion occupied a dominant position, and the coexistence of religions of diverse origins was a distinctive feature. In such a society, if separation of religion and government is not guarded especially strictly, there is great danger that freedom of religion would soon turn into a dead letter.

The establishing of both freedom of religion and separation of religion and government in the postwar Constitution was brought about due to the demands of international and domestic democratic influences. The fact that freedom of religion is guaranteed by means of a clear separation of religion and government is an extremely progressive feature for a Constitution of a capitalist country.

Buddhism's Postwar Readjustments

The fact that the land of the *kami* was defeated and the emperor renounced his divinity inevitably lowered the prestige of Shintō, Buddhism, and Christianity, all of which had openly cooperated in the war effort. After defeat, the leaders of these three religions accepted peace with deep repentance. Most Japanese, burned out of their homes during the war destruction and wandering about at the point of starvation, had lost faith and truly felt there were no *kami* or buddhas. Visits to Shintō shrines sharply declined and the Occupation forces publicly expressed their plans to convert Japan to Christianity. Both Buddhism and Sect Shintō, having lost their former privileges as officially recognized religions, were to grope for a new start.

Buddhist organizations received a severe blow from the democratization of Japan carried out under the Occupation. Buddhism lost its prestige, and its influence on the people declined. Extensive financial losses were made in various denominations and the hierarchical order within Buddhist organizations was shaken.

Living conditions in the immediate postwar years were difficult: As far as the eye could see, cities were scorched to the ground, and people were starving. Christian churches, which received the aid of the Occupation forces, engaged in such activities as relief for the homeless and distribution of relief materials. By contrast, the Buddhists were very inactive. Temples that were damaged during the war numbered 4,609 (about 6 percent of the total number of temples), most of these being city temples. Among smaller city temples, parishioners lived under trying circumstances, and in conditions where even maintenance of temples was difficult, it was almost impossible for these temples to turn their attention from religious services to social problems. But in the December following defeat, the Nihon Bukkyō Sankōkai (Japanese Buddhist Praise Society) started a street campaign raising funds for the relief of starving citizens; in July of the following year, with temples such as Sensōji in Tokyo serving as centers, they provided religious services and rice gruel to more than 8,000 people facing food shortages in Mikawashima and Tsukiji.

On the other hand, among the temples of rural villages where damages from the war were slight, the agrarian land reform made its impact with the promulgation of the Owner Farmers Establishment Special Measures Law (Jisakunō Sōsetsu Tokubetsu Sochi Hō) in October, 1946. It suddenly reduced the prewar financial foundation of the temples. The agrarian reform dissolved the landlord-tenant system, thereby suddenly transforming the structure of rural villages. This inevitably caused great changes in the system of small temples of such denominations as Shingon, Sōtō, Nichiren, and Jōdo, all of which were landowning temples. Furthermore, the power of the landlord class, which had supported the temples of rural villages, also declined, and even the sense of community of the villages, which gave moral support to the temples, began to diminish. Most small temples were so financially hard pressed that it became the practice for priests to take a second job to make a living. The agrarian reform did not deal with the distribution of mountain forests, and among the large temples which were denominational headquarters, although they were to dispose of their landholdings, some were allowed to retain their large boundaries. Therefore, among a few large temples the influence of the agrarian reform was slight, but these cases should be considered as exceptions.

Temples in prewar Japan relied completely on the family and its parishioner relationship to temples. In postwar times, in both cities and countryside, temples inevitably experienced essential changes due to the dissolution of the family system and the weakening of the sense of family. The priests of small temples took second jobs and became teachers, public employees, or started businesses in their homes. They also operated kindergartens and other social and educational enterprises by making use of the temple precincts and facilities. Established Buddhism's large priestly class gradually degenerated into performers of rituals, and the purpose and role of Buddhist organizations became meaningless. Within established organizations the fact that most of the priests, who had the actual authority for managing the temples, held some sort of second job, diminished their main religious activities, both qualitatively and quantitatively.

In established Buddhism in the early 1950s, there were some city temples which, because of the improved economic power of their influential parishioners, were able to enjoy a restoration of their influence. However, in general, the administration of both small urban and rural temples was still carried out under difficult conditions. The more popular temples, known for their special this-worldly benefits, and the temples which were famous tourist sites prospered with their large incomes. Especially the ancient temples in such places as Kyoto, Nara, and Kamakura, due to the growing tourist boom which accompanied the improved living standards of the middle class, became exhibition sites and custodians of cultural properties, rather than religious institutions. Among the large temples which had traditionally been headquarters temples, there was a trend toward developing tourism through such assistance as the capital of private railway companies.

Dispute and Reform Within Buddhism

With the abolition of the system of official recognition of religions, the prewar relationship between main and branch temples was radically altered. The control of religion, as practiced under the Religious Organizations Law, was almost abolished and there was a return to the former pattern with the restoration of the separation of religion and government under the Religious Corporations Ordinance. However, in the process of democratization under the Occupation, internal disputes intensified among the head priests of the main Buddhist organizations, and from lower ranks there was a movement for democratization of the organization. During the schisms due to internal disputes, in December, 1947, there was the secession of the main headquarters temple Chion-in from the Jōdo sect (forming the Jōdoshū Hompa). In the Sōto sect internal troubles continued until March, 1950. In the Nichiren sect in March, 1946, the headquarters temple Nakayama Hokekyōji seceded and founded the Nakayama Myō sect. In July of the same year, 120 temples seceded from the Kōyasan Shingon sect and created the Kūkai sect.

The separation and independence of powerful temples followed one after another. Soon after the war, in January, 1946, the temple Shitennōji seceded from the Tendai sect and founded the Wa sect. A number of other traditionally powerful temples also became independent: in March of the same year, the temple Shōgo-in (from Tendai sect to the Shugen sect); in July, 1947, the temple Kurama-dera (from Tendai sect to Kurama Kōkyō); in August, 1950, the temple Sensōji (from Tendai sect to Shōkannon sect); in November of the same year, the temple Hōryūji (from Hossō sect to Shōtoku sect).

These internal disputes and schisms of the Buddhist organizations reflected the weakening of the economic basis of established Buddhism. A more direct reason for the formation of independent denominations was the fact that they had become legally free, and the power struggles among religious administrators that had been taking place within Buddhist circles were thus exposed. The expectation and trust of the people toward organized Buddhism were betrayed even more by these internal disputes and schisms. The secession of powerful temples was conspicuous especially among the large temples of headquarters rank which were numerous in the Tendai denominations. Although doctrinal differences played a part in these schisms, the fact that the continued relationship of main and branch temples was considered a liability was a more decisive factor. The trend of the times also worked to the advantage of the development of new religions.

It would be difficult to state that the internal disputes of Buddhist organizations and the secession of powerful temples developed out of a deliberate criticism of the prewar Buddhist organizations, but the structural reform within religious organizations was a response to postwar democratization. The object of these reforms was the modernization of the organization itself. Positions such as chief abbot, which combined the office of religious and administrative authority, were abolished, and it became customary to have a system in which an official of the clergy (such as an abbot) and the administrator (such as a business manager) were separate people. Another noteworthy change is that an increasing number of denominations adopted systems of lay and priestly unity through the participation of lay believers in legislative assemblies for the organizational management. Thus during the Occupation, within both main branches of the Shinshū denominations, the Sōtō sect, the Nichiren sect, and among the other major denominations, the formal reform of religious systems was carried out on a wide scale. There was still a tendency to attempt to preserve the prewar structure of Buddhist organizations, and this was far removed from the true modernization of established Buddhism.

In the midst of the sudden transformation of postwar Japanese society, it was impossible to extricate oneself from reliance on political authorities. In the upheaval of the times and the poverty of branch temple priests, established Buddhism was in need of a reform from within. But Buddhist leaders retained their conservative position within the patriarchal emperor system, and until the clergy and believers could awaken to the original message of Buddhism, a reform movement could not begin. Under the Occupation, the movement to democratize Buddhist organizations had only slight concrete results at the time, but it exerted a great influence on the whole Buddhist world in the independent movement to reform the basic framework of organized Buddhism.

The movement to democratize Buddhist organizations developed in several directions, and from the Buddhist viewpoint, were progressive: structural reform, the determining of the responsibility of leading priests in the war, the formation of unions for priests at powerful temples and the improvement of working conditions of priests, and cooperation with various democratization movements outside of religion. What became the impetus for the movement were progressive priests and some individual Buddhists (priests acting on the basis of their Buddhist faith outside established Buddhism).

In July, 1946, the Buddhist Socialistic Alliance was formed by Senō Girō and Mibu Shōjun (1908–) (members of the prewar Newly Arisen Buddhist Youth Alliance), and in April, 1948, was renamed the Buddhist Social Alliance (Bukkyō Shakai Dōmei). The leading Buddhist priests during and after the war formed the Buddhist Federation (Bukkyō Rengōkai) in February, 1946, and released a document entitled "Plan for the Establishment of a New Japan by Buddhists" in May, 1947. Although they extolled peace in their "million-fold repentance," their actions betrayed their efforts to stem the democratization of Buddhist organizations. The Buddhist Social Alliance criticized this movement and advocated that Buddhism should reform its inflexible and antiquated basic framework and contribute to the democratic reform of Japanese society. In April, 1949, the Nationwide Alliance for the Reform of Buddhist Organizations (Zenkoku Bukkyō Kyōdan Kakushin Remmei) was formed, uniting movements for the democratization of Buddhist organizations in all denominations. This alliance sought to reform Buddhist organizations through large-scale participation of lay believers in the administrative agencies of each sect.

In June, 1954, the All-Japan Buddhist Association (Zen Nihon Bukkyō Kai) was formed as a federated body for all denominations, with 60-odd denominations participating. The All-Japan Conference of Buddhists (Zen Nihon Bukkyōtō Kyōkai) which was a deliberating body of the Buddhist movement for laymen and priests, which developed out of the universal Buddhist movement, also expanded its local organization and became active in its endeavors for social edification.

Competition Within Established Buddhism

In March and April of 1961, there were major memorial services
for Buddhist founders Hōnen and Shinran at such Kyoto temples
as Chion-in, Higashi Honganji, and Nishi Honganji; this provided an opportunity for Buddhist organizations to restructure
themselves and review their edification programs. Pilgrims to the
various sect headquarters during these memorials were reported
to be 380,000 at Chion-in, 520,000 at Nishi Honganji, and
850,000 at Higashi Honganji. Established Buddhist groups, pressured by competition from the new religions, put much energy
into the organization of the elaborate memorial services, as a sort
of demonstration of their latent capabilities. However, a large percentage of the worshipers were middle-aged and elderly people,
and from incidents, such as the exposure of disputes between main
temples and branch temples concerning the collection of contributions, the memorials rather demonstrated the limitations of the
large organizations of established Buddhism. As a result, various
denominations, such as the influential organizations of the Shinshū
Ōtani denomination, Sōtō sect, Jōdo sect, and Jōdo Shinshū Honganji denomination, sought improvement within their structures.
The Shinshū Ōtani denomination was having difficulties collecting
contributions for the memorial services and was recovering from
the damages that set it back in the 1959 Ise Bay typhoon. It
planned to establish a doctrine suitable to the times and a complete
change in its organizational structure. In June, 1962, the Dōbōkai
Undō, a movement to reform Buddhist sect organizations, was
inaugurated, and in place of the previous organizational structure
which relied on families and temples, a new one based on faith and
on small groups of believers was advanced.

In June, 1959, the Sōtō sect published its white paper on sect
strength and clarifed its organizational reform: it dealt with the
contradiction within the clericalism centered around traditional
priestly precepts and the actual secularized conditions. It aimed at
reform of the sect as a whole transcending the rivalry between the
two temples Eiheiji and Sōjiji since Meiji times, and such reforms
as the revision of branch-temple obligations were carried out.

Within the Jōdo Shinshū Honganji denomination, the reform of
religious systems under the Occupation ceased after 1948, and in

March, 1955, the Regulations for Assemblies, which followed the prewar system of temple order, were put into effect again. The organizational reform following the memorials brought the head-quarters and the mass of believers together, and by promoting sect consciousness they attempted to achieve concrete results in their program. In July, 1962, a "believers movement" was established, and in large cities, such as Tokyo and Osaka, it promoted a new start for its sect.

In the Jōdo sect, as a result of organizational fragmentation caused by the secession of Chion-in, the headquarters temple, a dispute over branch temples continued between the Jōdo sect (Jōdoshū) and the newly formed Jōdoshū Hompa. Prospects for reunification were improved by the concern of branch temple priests and their followers for the future of the organization; on the occasion of the memorials in 1961, unification was achieved with the formation of the Greater Jōdo sect, and organizational reforms were promoted.

Also, in the Myōshinji denomination of the Rinzai sect, the Hanazonokai became the impetus for structural improvement. Among various Shingon denominations, opportunities for co-operation, such as the association of headquarters temples (*hon-zankai*), were created and effective propagation was studied.

There was rivalry between organized Buddhist and Buddhist-derived new religions, but there was also a remarkable coopera-tive element in their relationship. For the new religions, their pres-tige was enhanced by becoming associated with the tradition of established Buddhism and their doctrinal teachings were enriched by such contact. For established Buddhism, by bringing the new religions under its jurisdiction as lay organizations, it meant re-gaining its influence over society.

Domestic and International Activities of Established Buddhism

The sociopolitical changes brought about by the Occupation's democratization policy influenced Buddhists denominations to reform their own structures. Urged on by the growth of the new religions and the stronger voice of Buddhist lay believers, a universal Buddhist movement developed, striving for the renewal of Buddhism beyond the framework of denominational Buddhism. The main force of this movement was in the individual Buddhists who were relatively free from established Buddhist groups. The Buddhist Federation, which was a confederacy of Buddhist denominations, also lent its assistance. In May, 1950, the first World Buddhist Conference was held at Colombo, Sri Lanka, one of Asia's newly independent Buddhist countries. Representatives from 25 countries, including Japan, participated. Buddhism's new developments, linked to the resurgence of folk culture within Buddhist countries of Southeast Asia, provided a great stimulus to Japanese Buddhism during the Occupation. Scheduling the second World Buddhist Conference to be held two years later in Japan, the universal Buddhism movement expanded on a full scale.

In April, 1951, the Conference of Japanese Buddhists was formed as a national body of priests and followers. There was tension between the independent individual Buddhists, who held influential positions in the universal Buddhist movement, and the leading priests of various denominations. Nevertheless, the second World Buddhist Conference was held in September and October of 1952 as the first large international religious conference to be held in Japan. From this point on, there was active interchange between Japan and Buddhist countries of Asia.

In the 1960s, such phenomena as the Zen boom and the reappraisal of Japanese Buddhism gradually aroused interest in Buddhism. Especially in the summer of 1962, a program called "Hitozukuri" was launched for the purpose of nurturing a future working class. The government made an unconstitutional stand by saying that religion was a necessary element in the development of the program. The authorities had thus committed themselves to the encouragement of religious education, and Buddhist organizations took the cue by beginning youth education programs. The All-Japan Youth Edification Conference (Zenkoku Shōnen Kyōka Kyōgikai) was established that year with the cooperation of priests of all denominations. Almost as if to counteract the propagation activities and youth organizations of the new religions, the temples made a conscientious effort to promote their social involvement through such activities as edification of youth and counselling services. But their programs were basically conservative in nature and only served to emphasize the premodern character of established Buddhism.

At the time of the 1960 citizens' movement against the U.S.-Japan Security Treaty, there was a political awakening among Buddhist groups as well, for Sōka Gakkai's entry into politics provided a stimulus, and they were approached by the conservative party as well. The All-Japan Buddhist Association established a socio-economic affairs committee in its sixth general meeting, but the association, as a federated organization of various sects, was restricted and therefore was unable to adopt a specific political program. On account of this, one group of denominational leaders and individual Buddhists in June, 1960, just at the time of the security treaty problem, formed the Buddhist Political Alliance (Bukkyō Seiji Dōmei). It embarked on political activities featuring the realization of politics based on Buddhism and opposition to communism. In spite of the fact that this movement was promoted in the form of an auxiliary organization to the All-Japan Buddhist Association, it floundered because it was unable to gain widespread support of established Buddhist organizations.

The Postwar Shintō Revivalist Movement

Within Shrine Shintō, the Association of Shintō Shrines, Jinja Honchō, organized about 78,000 shrines, constituting the majority of shrines nationwide; the other shrines were independent shrines or created small-scale federations of religious organizations, such as the Jinja Honkyō.

As an overall trend for Shrine Shintō, the decline of regional small shrines was remarkable, in contrast to the prosperity of the large shrines known for this-worldly benefits and those related to the imperial family, to which extensive grounds were given by the government almost at no cost. Shrines preserved their function as the local religion in farming villages, but as Shintō rites became formalized, there were many cases in which the Shintō priests did no more than carry out their role as performers of rituals. In the cities, the concentration of the population and migration severely weakened the people's sense of regional ties. However, it had been customary for shrines to be supported and maintained by influential people of a given locale. About 80 percent of 17,000 Shintō priests made their living by holding second jobs, such as teaching and office work. After the peace treaty in 1951, there was an active movement attempting to reconstitute the parish organization throughout farming villages and cities, but it became associated with the consolidation of a conservative political base.

Within Shintō organizations, there was also a movement to create a systematic doctrine turning Shintō into a world religion beyond its traditional framework as a folk religion, but this was unsuccessful. In the early 1950s, the Shintō leaders mounted a reactionary movement for the revival of State Shintō. For the majority of small shrines, which did not have strong ties with the lives of the people and which were poor in revenue, this provided a pragmatic basis for fantasizing the dream of reinstating the special privileges they received under the State Shintō system.

In November, 1952, to set the tone of revivalism, rites installing the crown prince were performed. The following year, at the cost of two billion yen, Ise Shrine was rebuilt, a ritual rebuilding carried out every twenty years but which had been delayed due to the war. For Shintō, the occasion suddenly heightened the opportunity for restoration.

Under the the system of the U.S.-Japan security treaty, Japan was able to restore monopoly capitalism and rapid economic growth. In the late 1950s, the reactionary trend of politics steadily intensified, and in the area of religion both the freedom of religion and the democratic principle of separation of government and religion were openly violated. To a certain degree, the control of religion according to regulations of the former Religious Organizations Law was restored.

In 1959, the government treated the Shintō rite Kashikodokoro Omae no Gi, a formal announcement to the *kami* in the imperial palace, in the wedding of the crown prince, as a state affair. Then in 1960 in the prime minister's speech to the Diet, he recognized the proprietary rights of the Imperial Household over Ise Shrine's object of worship, *yata no kagami*.[1] In 1963, government-sponsored nationwide memorial rites for the war dead were performed on

---

[1] *Yata no kagami*, the mirror which according to tradition was given by the Sun Goddess to her grandson as one of the three sacred regalia symbolizing the imperial right to rule Japan.

August 15th, the anniversary of surrender, and the rites thereafter became state ceremonies observed annually. These rites, which memorialized the war dead as "fallen heroes defending the state" and in which the emperor and empress participated, together with the practice of conferring decorations on the war dead, which began the following year, were means of reviving militaristic thought.

The nationalization of Ise Shrine and Yasukuni Shrine is considered a major breakthrough in the movement to restore State Shintō. Ise Shrine, which venerates the ancestor *kami* of the emperor and which was directly related to the emperor, is the virtual head of all shrines. The change to national administration of Ise Shrine would bring about the restoration of the official state character of Shrine Shintō and would mean reviving the divine character of the emperor.

As for Yasukuni Shrine, which had played a large role in the dissemination of militarism, under the Occupation even its continued existence had been uncertain. In 1963 and thereafter, there were successive publicized plans for state maintenance of Yasukuni Shrine. This was related to a plan to make Yasukuni Shrine a special juridical person over which the emperor would preside. These were attempts to preserve the prewar militaristic structure and at the same time legitimize state participation through the theory that shrines are non-religious. This reactionary movement was supported by right-wing members of the ruling Liberal Democratic Party, right-wing organizations, local veterans' associations, associations of families of dead soldiers, the Association of Shintō Shrines, and such religious organizations as Seichō no Ie and Kokuchūkai. On the whole, this tendency received the support of the government and the party in power.

In 1967, in spite of the opposition from all classes of people, the prewar Empire Day, Kigensetsu, celebrated on February 11, was restored as Kenkoku Kinenbi, National Foundation Day. Thus, in education, too, an unscientific mythical education was introduced.

Participation in the Peace Movement

From the 1951 San Francisco Peace Treaty to the renewal of the U.S.-Japan Security Treaty of 1960, Japan experienced a revival of militarism which was supported by rapid economic growth. The government poured out its energies both against communism and for the elevation of its status as a major power. While the reactionary government stance became more and more obvious, in contrast, the progressive political parties were in the forefront of a popular citizens' movement to defend democracy and pacifism as established in the postwar Constitution. During the latter half of the Occupation period, around 1950, the intensification of the Cold War threatened the world with a third world war, and a worldwide peace movement began. In such events as the inauguration of the Gandhi Peace Alliance in January, 1950, and the formation of the Roundtable of Religionists at Kyoto in April of the same year, progressive Buddhists became a major force in the peace movement. But it was in June, 1950, when the Korean War broke out and the question of the rearming of Japan became a reality that religious groups became earnest in their participation in the movement. Buddhists cooperated with Christian and other religious movements. The Buddhists based their movement on their precept not to take life. The Protestant peace activists formed the Christians' Peace Association. In February, 1951, the Buddhists' Peace Roundtable was started, and in June, when the Religionists' Peace Movement Conference was convened, became its affiliated body. This conference was supported by some clergy and laymen of Buddhism, Christianity, and the new religions, and supported universal peace and opposed rearmament. Although it was a minor force within the religious world as a whole, for the first time it brought about the cooperation of labor unions and political parties, and it was responsible for the development of the international peace movement. In July, together with the General Council of Trade Unions of Japan, it created the People's Conference for the Promotion of Peace.

In 1954, a Japanese fisherman died of radioactive fallout from a U.S. hydrogen bomb test at Bikini Atoll, making the first victim of the hydrogen bomb a Japanese citizen. The anger and grief of the nation found form in the appeal for a ban on atomic and hydrogen bombs and spread to religious groups also. Ōmoto-kyō and Jinrui Aizenkai, which had promoted the movement for a world federation, took the initiative on a worldwide scale, acquiring 1,600,000 signatures appealing for a ban on bombs. Statements opposing the bombs were also issued from other religious organizations.

Through the movement to ban atomic and hydrogen bombs, which expanded on a worldwide scale, exchange with foreign religious peace movements were made anew. From 1953, the repatriation of the remains of Chinese prisoners of war, who had been victims of Japanese wartime forced marches, was begun, thereby deepening the friendship and interchange between the Buddhists groups of Japan and China. There was also some interchange with Southeast Asian countries.

The denominations of the Nichiren sect developed a movement for establishing righteousness and peace.[2] Nihonzan Myōhōji, the new religion which lost its following in China after the war, abandoned its wartime chauvinism and support for the Greater East East Asia Co-prosperity Sphere and developed doctrine based on absolute peace and non-violence adopted from the thought of Gandhi. Together with Ōmoto-kyō, it assumed the leadership of the Religion and Peace Movement. The yellow-robed priests and lay believers of Nihonzan Myōhōji beat their hand drums and loudly chanted the *daimoku*[3] as they participated in the peace movement. Out of their belief in nationalism and absolute peace, they also joined the movement opposing foreign military bases in Japan. They entered the land at Sunagawa proposed for the expansion of the U.S. Air Base in Tachikawa, and their priests were attacked and seriously wounded by the police.[4] Maruyama-kyō, which was derived from a Fuji cult, had also cooperated in the war effort, but it too came to devote its efforts to the peace movement.

The peace movement spread among such religious organizations as Konkō-kyō, Sekai Kyūsei-kyō, Tenri-kyō, Shugenshū, and Hommon Butsuryūshū. The movement was not proposing an abstract ideal of peace; it faced the realities of Japan, and sought concrete means to protect peace.

---

[2] Risshō Heiwa Undō seems to be derived from Nichiren's popular slogan *risshō ankoku*, establishment of righteousness and security of the country.

[3] *Daimoku*, the title of the Lotus Sutra, invoked as a prayer of magical power.

[4] The "Sunagawa Incident" led to a protracted series of court cases not only concerning prosecution of these "trespassers," but also touching on the legality of foreign military bases in Japan and the constitutionality of the Security Treaty.

At the Japanese Conference of World Pacifists convened in April, 1954, the efforts of the Japanese Religion and Peace Movement were regarded as important contributions to the international peace movement.

The opposition to the renewal of the Security Treaty in the summer of 1960 became the largest postwar national movement. The government urged the leadership of Buddhism, the new religions, and Christianity to support the signing of the Security Treaty, and planned to invite the new religions' membership to the welcome for President Eisenhower on his proposed visit to Japan. Most religious organizations supported the Security Treaty, but Sōka Gakkai proclaimed its neutrality. Ōmoto-kyō, Nihonzan Myōhōji, Maruyama's Peace Association, the Nichiren sect's Puruna Association, the Christian Peace Association, and many other religious organizations and religionists opposed the Security Treaty. A diversified spontaneous movement grew in activities such as collecting opposition signatures, demonstrations exclusively by religionists, and hunger strikes by priests.

The anti–Security Treaty movement provided a stimulus to Ōmoto-kyō's overture to peace. Confronted with the reality of Japan's reactionary trend, it became involved in the movement to defend the postwar peace Constitution. It collected 7,480,000 signatures supporting the spirit of the Constitution and seeking total world disarmament.

In July, 1961, the World Religionists' Peace Conference was convened at Kyoto with foreign representatives including those from socialist countries participating. They released the Kyoto declaration urging a "coming together of inner peace and world peace." Prompted by this world conference, in April of the next year the Japanese Religionists' Peace Conference was formed, and in July, 1964, the second World Religionists' Peace Conference was held at Tokyo.

On the other hand, in contrast to the development of the progressive Religion and Peace Movement, there was a peace movement which advocated anti-communism. Groups such as the Association of Shintō Shrines and the new religions in the Union of New Religious Organizations of Japan (Shin Nihon Shūkyō Dantai Rengōkai), especially Risshō Kōseikai, which was the driving force in the movement for religious cooperation. In 1963, Matsushita Masatoshi (1901-) of the Anglican Church and leaders of other religious organizations formed the Religion and Peace Mission to Ban Nuclear Weapons, and visited the Vatican and various European countries.

13. New Religions in the Postwar Era

The Occupation's policy of democratization from above rapidly retreated in the midst of the upheaval of world conditions —the intensification of the Cold War between the Soviet Union and the United States, the establishment of Communist China following the success of the Chinese revolution, and the independence of Asian and African countries. The outbreak of the Korean War started a whole chain of reactionary policies beginning with the rearmament of Japan. Japanese capitalism entered a period of resurgence supported by the emergency demands of the Korean War, with the strength of monopolistic capitalism being renewed. Democratization during the Occupation and the democratic movement which arose within the confusion of postwar society demanded the essential transformation of religion's basic character. Disorganization of the family, permeation of the scientific rationality, and an enhanced democratic movement all furthered the trend of indifference toward religion. Established Buddhism and Shrine Shintō as a whole lost much of their influence, but the propagation of Christianity received the assistance of the Occupation Force and prospered.

Many foreign Catholic and Protestant missionaries learned of the Occupation Force's plan to convert Japan to Christianity and came to Japan, bringing with them money and relief materials. The Catholics addressed themselves to the imperial family, and for a while there were rumors of the conversion of the imperial family to Catholicism. In 1949, the whole village of Saga near Kyoto converted to Catholicism, but the conversion was motivated by a wish to acquire relief materials, and in later years apostates were to emerge. Within the Orthodox Church, the main group up to this time, a derivative of the Russian Orthodox group, was driven

137

out of control, and in 1946, the year after defeat, an alliance was formed with the Orthodox Church of America, but an internal dispute between the two groups was to continue thereafter.

Protestants had declined in numbers during the wartime oppression, but during the Occupation aid from foreign countries continued to flow to the United Church of Christ in Japan and other denominations. They were active in the area of cultural and social affairs, and in such programs as the distribution of two million copies of the Bible. However, in the context of a democratized Japan, Christianity failed to attract followers beyond its traditional intellectual and upper-class members. New members rapidly increased, reaching a peak in 1947, and thereafter leveled off.

The Resurgence of Popular Religions

The religions that most attracted the people after the war were overwhelmingly the new religions which centered on this-worldly benefits. The new religions offered a salvation that answered the deeply rooted aspirations of the people. Traditional magic and shamanism maintained the belief in this-worldly benefits and miracles.

The sects of Shintō, which formed the original currents of new religions, up to this time had been categorized under Sect Shintō as officially recognized religions, but following the war, affiliation to this artificial system of State Shintō was abolished. Tenri-kyō under the leadership of the patriarch Nakayama Shozen (1905–67) promoted the "restoration to the original state" movement, a return to the spirit of the founder. Konkō-kyō's internal disputes had continued into the wartime period, and with the defeat it celebrated its liberation, for it was able for the first time to display the original doctrine of its founder as a living *kami*. In 1949, it initiated a "movement for a life of devotion completed through intercession (*toritsugi*)," and sought to rebuild its religious strength. In 1946, Ōmoto-kyō was renamed Aizen'en. Deguchi Onisaburō considered the fact that he had not participated in the war effort to be divine will. He said that the *kami* had saved Ōmoto-kyō for the next age. The oppressive imperial state system and its myths had collapsed, and fascism was, in the end, unable to overthrow the faith of popular religions.

Jikōson and the Dancing Religion

In January, 1946, as if to respond to the emperor's declaration of his humanity, Kumazawa Hiromichi (1888–1966), a shopkeeper living in Nagoya, announced himself as the legitimate emperor of the southern court.[1] The matter was reported in the Occupation Force's newspaper *Stars and Stripes* and became a topic of conversation. Kumazawa originally was a priest of the Sōtō sect who claimed that from previous ages the southern court was legitimate, but due to the abolition of the crime of *lèse majesté* he could now emphasize publicly his right of imperial succession.

In January of the next year, the same general conditions of disorder prevailed, and the religion of Jiu-kyō predicted natural calamities; Jiu-kyō created a "cabinet" with former wrestling champion Futabayama and chess champion Go Seigen as "cabinet members." The leaders of Jiu-kyō were arrested at the end of a disturbance in Kanazawa under suspicion of infringement of the food control laws. The founder Nagaoka Yoshiko (1903–), called Jikōson, belonged to the line of Asano Wasaburō's (1873–1935) Spiritualist Research Association (Shinrei Kagaku Kenkyūkai), which had split from Ōmoto-kyō. Nagaoka argued that Amaterasu Ōmikami had left the emperor when he had declared his humanity and had entered Jikōson. In order to realize a world renewal of "the way of *kami* and people" (*shimmindō*) she had organized her "cabinet."

In August, 1945, just before the war ended, Kitamura Sayo (1900–67), the wife of a farmer, established her own religion Tenshō Kōtai Jingū-kyō.[2] After the war, she became popular for the sermons she sang in which she said the emperor was a cast-off shell, denouncing the people as maggots and rejecting the established authorities. Kitamura had suffered greatly under the feudalistic family system. Studying under an Inari practitioner, she was possessed by *kami*, and during the war she came to the realization that a *kami* had entered her abdomen. Under the *kami's* instruc-

[1] See p. 67n.
[2] Tenshō is another pronunciation for Amaterasu, and Kōtai Jingū means Ise Shrine.

tions, she began preaching on the streets of Tabuse, Yamaguchi Prefecture. With the defeat of Japan, the land of the *kami*, Kitamura claimed to be the only child of the *kami* and a savior (*kyūseisha*) and propagated her faith. Seichō no Ie and Nichiren teachings influenced the doctrine of Tenshō Kōtai Jingū-kyō. In September, 1948, she went to Sukiyabashi in Tokyo and led her dance of "selflessness"[3] through group ecstasy. This earned them the name of "dancing religion" (*odoru shūkyō*).

Hommichi, Seichō no Ie, and Sekai Kyūsei-kyō

Hommichi's Ōnishi Aijirō was released as a political prisoner immediately after the war, and in 1946 he reconstituted Hommichi at Hagoromo near Osaka.

Seichō no Ie abruptly changed its wartime praise of fascism and the emperor, to a position supporting freedom. It renewed its modern trappings through such tactics as adopting spiritual analysis and psychosomatic medicine from the United States. In doctrine it promised the subjugation of human suffering and a life of prosperity. Transcending all religions and worshiping life itself, it urged the establishment of a heaven on earth by means of cooperation and mutual love. While its modern aspects became prominent, Seichō no Ie still promoted its Shintō and conservative character, and developed as a popular right-wing religious movement.

Okada Mokichi, who like Taniguchi Masaharu had left Ōmoto-kyō, reconstituted the Dainihon Kannon Kyōdan (Greater Japan Kannon Association) in 1947, reorganizing it as Sekai Meshiya-kyō, World Messiah Religion (later the Sekai Kyūsei-kyō, Church of World Messianity). Okada inherited the doctrine of Ōmoto-kyō and spread the teachings of both the faith healing of *jōrei* (purification of the spirit), which viewed medicine as poison, and also natural farming methods without fertilizer. This cultivation without fertilizer was welcomed by the farmers who suffered from a shortage of fertilizer at a time of increased food production. Okada was called Ohikarisamae ("venerable light") and was considered

---

[3] "Selflessness," *muga;* originally a Buddhist term meaning non-self or non-ego (*anātman* in Sanskrit), but here transformed by Kitamura into an eclectic and popular practice of losing the self in the ecstasy of dance.

a living *kami* who possessed a jewel called *nyōi-hoshu*[4] in his abdomen. Okada in his unpretentious sermons charmed his believers, promising them a society free of sickness, poverty, and war. Okada was a typical founder in the boom of new religions during the Occupation. Sekai Kyūsei-kyō developed rapidly under the Occupation and established a "heaven on earth" (*chijō tengoku*) under the names of Shinsenkyō at Gōra near Hakone, and Zuiunkyō at Atami. Okada was an antique dealer in the Asakusa area of Tokyo, and being confident of his judgment of art objects, he used the religion's funds and established an art museum at Hakone and Atami. In 1950, the religion was raided for tax evasion and bribery, and Okada was imprisoned. The propagation of Sekai Kyūsei-kyō—which openly rejected modern science and believed in miracles—was strongly criticized by the public. However, Okada had a unique ability to organize and lead people, and he established religious strength throughout the nation.

Hito no Michi Becomes PL Kyōdan

In 1946, Hito no Michi Kyōdan, which had dissolved under suppression during the war, started anew in Tosu, Saga Prefecture, as PL Kyōdan (later Perfect Liberty Kyōdan). There were earlier plans for the name to be "permanent" liberty, but it was changed to "perfect," in order to avoid confusion with permanent waves in hairdressing. The leader was Miki Tokuchika, who, wearing American-style clothes appropriate for the new age, swept out the Shintō nuances of Hito no Michi, at every opportunity amply using foreign words, such as "master," and expanding his religious territory by sponsoring social dances for his propagation. PL Kyōdan taught that life is art, and elaborating its individualistic and realist philosophy of life, organized a large following from the lower managerial class and salaried men of the cities of western Japan. In PL Kyōdan religion is considered an art, and in its individualistic and pragmatic outlook is seen the influence of Shingon esotericism dating back to PL Kyōdan's forerunner, Tokumitsu-kyō. PL Kyōdan's notion of life, typical of people of small towns was embraced by intellectuals and students as well.

[4] *Nyoi-hōshu*, a Buddhist term (*cintāmaṇi* in Sanskrit) meaning a fabulous gem or relic, but in this case something like the essence of Okada's divine, charismatic powers.

Ennō-kyō and Zenrinkai

Ennō-kyō in Hyōgo Prefecture is a new religion founded by Fukada Chiyoko (1887–1925) in 1919, who had been influenced by Tenri-kyō and Shugendō, and herself was possessed by *kami*. Under the postwar leadership of Fukada Chōji (1908–76), her son, this group's religious strength grew in the Kansai area.

Tenchi Kōdō Zenrinkai (later Zenrinkai) led by Rikihisa Tatsusai (1906–77) and centered in northern Kyūshū, also established a following. This new religion began with the spiritual experiences of Rikihisa Tatsusaburō, Tatsusai's father, who had been an evangelist of Jikkō-kyō during the Taishō era. In doctrine it valued the most important principles of life and emphasized spiritual training and the this-worldly benefit of healing. It was believed that the body and clothing of Zenrinkai's leader had the spiritual power of healing.

The Development of Reiyūkai

Seichō no Ie, Sekai Kyūsei-kyō, and PL Kyōdan were new religions that derived their doctrines from Shintō and other religions, but in the postwar years, derivatives of the Lotus tradition comprised the majority of the new religions: Reiyūkai in the early period of the Occupation, and from the latter period, lay movements such as Risshō Kōseikai, became increasingly popular.

Reiyūkai, which had linked together ancestor worship and the virtues of the Lotus Sutra, expanded its religious strength among farm villages of eastern Japan during the war. After the war, it reopened its guidance movement, urging "righteousness of thought and edification of society." Reiyūkai spread rapidly among the masses who sensed the crisis of the collapse of the family system and who were anxious at the prospects of a life of financial difficulties. It organized large numbers of housewives and businessmen whose common denominator was their conservative reliance on the family system. By 1948, with believers numbering 300,000 households, they were the largest new religion to develop during the Occupation. In 1950, Reiyūkai was exposed for tax evasion and possession of narcotics. During the leadership of President Kotani Kimi, the organization's internal disputes were unceasing. Starting with the separation of Miyamoto Mitsu's (1900–) group as Myōchikai in 1950, other schisms also formed: Sekiguchi Kaichi's (1897–1961) group as Bussho Gonenkai, Yamaguchi Giichi's group as Seigikai Kyōdan, Sahara Chūjirō's group as Myōdōkai. In 1953, Reiyūkai was investigated again, this time under suspicion of such crimes as bribery and of embezzling one million yen from a Red Feather collection campaign, and Kotani was arrested. The believers besieged the police in a united effort against what they considered religious persecution.

The Development of Risshō Kōseikai

Risshō Kōseikai, which before the war had separated from Reiyūkai, although it inherited from Reiyūkai the teachings of ancestor worship, was distinctive in its emphasis on the perfection of the individual self. Risshō Kōseikai's development was the most conspicuous of all new religions during the Occupation period. It was successful in organizing large numbers of urban housewives by means of discussion groups called *hōza*.[5] Risshō Kōseikai developed its teachings in the direction of perfecting the individual self through the realization of altruistic actions. It forwarded a new kind of character out of an awareness of the breakdown of the family system; the keynote for this character was based on a morality of conservative personal restraint, phrased in such terms as "a humble spirit."

Risshō Kōseikai, centered in eastern Japan, entered a period of nationwide expansion during the latter part of the Occupation. It increased rapidly from a publicly announced number of 310,000 believers in 1951 to 1,040,000 in 1955. Risshō Kōseikai's large development depended greatly on the utilization of the *hōza* organization as an opportune situation for consultation, persuasion, and learning. Its teaching linked the theories of various folk beliefs (such as astrology, calendrical omens, directional divination, and onomancy) with a unique theory of causation based on the virtues of the Lotus Sutra. It also drew upon traditional folk magic and shamanistic rites. Vice President Naganuma Myōkō attracted the faith of believers, who considered her a living buddha (*ikibotoke*), and President Niwano Nikkyō systematized the doctrine.

---

[5] *Hōza*, literally Buddhist law (*dharma*, or *hō*) discussion; as the text indicates, its actual practice is more person-centered than doctrinal.

Other New Religions

Myōchikai and Myōdōkai, both derived from Reiyūkai, developed religious strength locally in the latter part of the Occupation. Among the Buddhist-derived new religions were the Tendai-derived Nempōshin-kyō and Kōdō Kyōdan, the Shingon-derived Gedatsukai, Itō Shinjō's (1906–) Shinnyo-en, and Yasaka Kakushō's Nakayamashingo-shōshū, each developing distinctive activities on a local scale. Also, there were the organizations formed from the pilgrim associations (kō) of influential temples (connected to established Buddhism through such avenues as isson shinkō, belief in a specific buddha or kami, and sangaku shinkō, or religious practices in the mountains), and the new organizations born out of schisms from established Buddhist organizations: these constituted a large percentage of the Buddhist-derived new religions out of the total number of organizations. Furthermore, there appeared new religions which featured syncretistic doctrine drawn from such sources as Shintō, Taoism, and Confucianism, and added this to the foundation of Buddhist doctrine.

Among the Buddhist-derived new religions which continued to develop after the peace treaty of 1951 were Ogura Reigen's (1886–) Nempōshin-kyō centered in Osaka, and Kōdō Kyōdan in Yokohama. Nempōshin-kyō featured a doctrine based on the revelation of Amida. It attracted its membership through magical this-worldly benefits. Kōdō Kyōdan, which had split from Reiyūkai before the war, and was based on faith in the Lotus Sutra and had religious exchanges with Buddhists in Sri Lanka.

Postwar Society and the New Religions

The large new organizations—such as Sekai Kyūsei-kyō, PL Kyōdan, Reiyūkai, and Risshō Kōseikai—which during the Occupation developed their religious strength, carried out their propagation activities relying on remarkably irrational and premodern methods of magical this-worldly benefits. Their attitude toward political and social problems was conservative or indifferent. The popularity of new religions and their astonishing development invited society's criticism, particularly for their magical, commercial, and reactionary character. There were also new religions that were registered as religious juridical persons but which operated mainly as profit-making enterprises. For example, in 1949, an association of small organizations called Kōdō Chi-kyō was exposed. Also, under the Organizations Control Ordinance, the Shintōderived small organizations, such as Ishin Remmei and Tenshinkyo, were ordered to disband due to their extremely nationalistic doctrine.

Under the Religious Corporations Ordinance of 1947, the new religions numbered 207, counting only the nationwide organizations derived from Shintō, Buddhism, and other religions. However, by the time the 1951 Religious Juridical Persons Law was put into effect, the number had reached 720.

Behind the explosive expansion of the new religions were the great changes in postwar social conditions. Many of the new religions were independent popular religious movements which developed under the prewar system of official recognition of religions. With defeat and the abolition of the control of religion, for the first time they were able to freely carry out their propagation activities without concern for government oppression or interference. The realization of freedom of religion was the greatest external factor in the development of the new religions. Furthermore, the decline in prestige and diminished social functions of the established religions created favorable conditions for the growth of the new religions. As is clear from the fact that large established Buddhist organizations themselves pursued a course of organizational renewal through the participation of lay believers in administrative matters, leadership in the Buddhist movement increasingly tended to shift from the clergy (who by the very nature of their profession maintained a certain distance from social life) to laymen who had their own professions. The new religions were supported by these social conditions, and they expanded their active propagation, claiming the image of an ideal world free of sickness, poverty, and war by means of this-worldly benefits directly related to life and work, such as healing of the sick, prosperity in business, harmony in one's family, or a new purpose in living. The new religions, because of contradictions and lack of systemization in doctrine and their unabashed use of magic and shamanism in their propagation, were held in contempt by the established religions, intellectuals, and journalists. However, the new religions drew believers and seekers, organized them into small discussion groups, and through consultation and persuasion directly met the religious needs of the masses, embracing the believers in terms of their total lives. Before long the believers who had experienced these religious benefits turned into lay evangelists, and by means of propagation activities they dealt with contradictions between their lives and minds. In this way, by providing their own solutions, they contributed revisions to doctrinal content by adding lessons learned through evangelistic practices.

At the time of the desolation and poverty during the Occupation, and in the background of the intensification of social contradictions accompanying the resurgence of monopolistic capitalism during the Korean War that followed, the new religions, through their doctrine and organizational formation, found their place in the life of the people, overtook the position of the established religions, and efficiently performed the social function of religion in a capitalist society: inner salvation for individuals. The main foundation of the postwar new religions shifted greatly from the middle and lower classes of farm villages to the lower salaried class and the middle and lower managerial class. The organizations' leadership in many cases was in the hands of the middle and lower managerial class, such that it made it difficult to break away from the political and intellectual conservatism of the organizations. The new religions which possessed religious strength on a nationwide scale were movements that through actual propagation aimed at the realization of a conceptual or real ideal world. Their structures were flexible, thus allowing themselves to adapt to society's unceasing changes. As an inevitable result of this basic framework, it can be said that in many cases the large new religions, in comparison with the uncompromising conservatism of the established organizations, expressed a more flexible form of political conservatism.

14. The Political Advance of Sōka Gakkai

Japan from the Korean War to the 1951 San Francisco Peace Treaty underwent drastic changes in its social structure that accompanied the rapid resurgence and strengthening of monopoly capitalism. The farming village population, with their backward ways, immigrated to large cities with their unfamiliar modernized view of life, shaking from its foundation the value system which had been based on the family and communal ties. Established Buddhism, which preserved its position as a religion of the family, continued its decline nationwide and was unable to regain its influence over the people, in spite of the relative prosperity of Buddhism's powerful supporting class—middle- and upper-class farmers, the urban middle class, and the managerial class—accompanying the rapid growth of industry. The nationwide expansion of the religious strength of the new religions from the Occupation period onward made it impossible to call them a socially unique phenomena. Within Japanese society, which welcomed the age of freedom of religion, prewar State Shintō's interference in the new religions' development disappeared. Although there was some prosperity and decline among individual new religions, as a whole they continued their development consistently after the war. The main organizations among the new religions in 1951, preceding the conclusion of peace in 1951, formed the Union of New Religious Organizations of Japan. It is no exaggeration to say that in the 1950s the main strength of religious movement in Japan actually shifted to the new religions. Following the growth of Risshō Kōseikai, the new religion Sōka Gakkai, which also was derived from the tradition of the Lotus Sutra, entered a period of nationwide growth and in a decade grew into Japan's foremost large-scale religious organization.

147

The Organizational Development of Sōka Gakkai

In 1946, Toda Jōsei gathered together the old members of Sōka Kyōiku Gakkai, and under the name of Sōka Gakkai he rebuilt the organization. Through lectures on the Lotus Sutra, Toda was earnest in educating the young company employees and workers he assembled in Sōka Gakkai, and trained them in the practice of aggressive proselytism. Within Sōka Gakkai, in its process of rebuilding, energetic young men, such as Ikeda Daisaku (1928–), were brought up, and starting out in Tokyo they carried out their aggressive proselytism activities throughout the whole Kantō area, eventually acquiring 3,000 households of believers, close to the prewar peak membership.

In 1951, the year the peace treaty was negotiated, Toda took office as Sōka Gakkai's second president. Fearing the outbreak of a third world war and prompted by the intensification of the Korean War, Toda proclaimed a major campaign of forced conversion to "save Japan to save Asia." Toda created men's and women's youth corps as Sōka Gakkai's operational organization. The smallest organizational unit, the discussion group, or *zadankai* (which is a circle for the practice of aggressive proselytism and study of doctrine), was made the basis on which their efficient central administration for propagation was established: main headquarters, branch headquarters, regions, squads, and groups.

Toda called the *daigohonzon* (a mandala which was the central object of worship in Taisekiji, the head temple of Nichiren Shōshū) "the device for producing happiness"; he insisted that if one believes in the mandala, one will gain this-worldly benefits, such as healing of sickness and amassing of wealth. The theory of a national Buddhist altar (*Kokuritsu Kaidan*), which Nichiren Shōshū traditionally handed down, meant the realization of an ideal world in which there would be a unity of government and Buddhism and conversion of the entire world (*kōsen rufu*) through the conversion of the emperor. However, in Sōka Gakkai the theory was revised to mean that this would be realized through total conversion of the masses. Urging a sense of mission for this total conversion upon its believers, Sōka Gakkai developed an organized attack, denouncing all other religions as heresies. In actuality Sōka Gakkai controlled Nichiren Shōshū, with its tradition dating back to medieval times;

and they invested in the president of Sōka Gakkai, by means of the abbot of Nichiren Shōshū, the religious prestige of the True Buddha, or Nichiren. In this manner, a structure was established in which the leadership of their president possessed absolute authority both religiously and secularly. The religion expanded from the Tokyo-Yokohama industrial region to all of the Kantō area, northeast Japan, Kansai, Kyūshū, and Hokkaidō. Middle- and lower-rank managers, unorganized laborers, housewives, farmers, and even organized laborers became believers.

The rapid resurgence and strengthening of monopoly capitalism intensified the systematizing of medium- and small-scale industry, subjecting the middle and lower ranks of the managerial class to severe fluctuations in their business. Workers in these smaller industries led unstable lives, and the degree of their poverty intensified. By acquiring as its main foundation the lower salaried class and the middle and lower ranks of the managerial class of large cities, Sōka Gakkai rapidly expanded. The characteristic feature of its doctrine was its combination of the world renewal aspiration for overthrow of the status quo and realization of an ideal world with magical this-wordly benefits. Through this ideology, Sōka Gakkai was able to build on the dissatisfaction and distrust of politics characteristic of the classes forming its base and their common resistance to progressive parties.

Sōka Gakkai strengthened its attack on other religions with military-style youth groups taking the lead; while others criticized it as a "violent" religion, Sōka Gakkai steadily expanded its religious strength. In the early 1950s, in a time when Sōka Gakkai entered a period of nationwide development, the established religions, such as Shrine Shintō and Buddhism, did experience a partial revival, but on the whole it was difficult to conceal their decline in influence on society.

Sōka Gakkai's Aggressive Tactics

The advance of the new religions gradually undermined the position of established Buddhism, but most of the new religions did not necessarily oppose the parish ties which through ancestor worship bound families to temples. In contrast to established

Buddhism with its formalism and its inactive propagation, the new religions developed their propagation centered on this-worldly benefits directly related to the daily lives of the people. There was no real need for the new religions to directly confront established Buddhism.

However, in the 1950s the propagation activities of Sōka Gakkai, which had expanded remarkably as a religious force, greatly altered the peaceful coexistence between the new religions and established Buddhism. Sōka Gakkai's doctrine claimed that Nichiren Shōshū was the unique, absolutely "True Buddhism" (shō-bō) and denounced all other religions as heresies, a fact which was the source of the people's misfortune. Sōka Gakkai launched a systematic attack of aggressive proselytism against the Nichiren sect as well as all the sects of established Buddhism. Sōka Gakkai's attack on established Buddhism was a challenge to sectarian disputes, and at the same time that it lashed out at Buddhism's doctrinal contradictions, it proceeded to mercilessly expose established Buddhism's secularization and commercialization, as well as its parasitic reliance on the people. This attack even called forth some sympathy from the nation which already harbored mistrust of established Buddhism.

There were sectarian disputes such as the Otaru dialogues held in Otaru, Hokkaidō, between Sōka Gakkai and the Nichiren sect in March, 1955, but following these, doctrinal criticism of Sōka Gakkai by the various sects of established Buddhism was intensified. Sōka Gakkai's aggressive proselytism created extreme tension between Sōka Gakkai and established Buddhism as new converts cut off their former parish ties and became members of Nichiren Shōshū. This was expressed in its most radical form in the dispute surrounding the litigation over burial in cemeteries.

This dispute arose when temples, which had traditionally buried members of their parish families, refused to bury those who had left the parish to join Sōka Gakkai. From the latter half of 1959, this became a problem throughout the country. Sōka Gakkai was supported by a notification from the Health Division of the Welfare Ministry that held that as cemeteries were public, the burials were proper. The temple insisted that burial was inseparable from religious ceremonies. A number of disputes were taken to court, and in February, 1962, the Civil Affairs Division of the Tokyo

District Court rejected a suit by the temples seeking to cancel the ruling of the Welfare Ministry. But the Bureau of Legislation interpreted the opinion of the Welfare Ministry in favor of established Buddhism: if burial of remains and religious ceremonies are separable, then religious organizations managing cemeteries, when there is a legitimate reason—except for the reason that the petitioner is a member of another religious organization—can refuse burial.

The cemetery dispute, as a direct challenge to the traditional authority of temples supported by a sense of communal ties, especially in the temples of farming villages, became a major problem for established Buddhism. However, the leadership of the Buddhist organizations still did not sense the urgent crisis in the growth of Sōka Gakkai and the new religions. Generally the gap in social function between established Buddhism and the new religions was so great that established Buddhism apparently did not consider them to be so serious a threat as one might imagine them to be. In the process of its growth since 1951, Sōka Gakkai organized the large urban salaried class and youth, and the direct impact exerted on temple administration as such, in both urban and rural areas, was not that great. For the temples, it amounted only to some parishioners with relatively weak economic ties to the temple separating themselves from the temple, and this did not threaten the temples' existence as such. For the established Buddhist organizations, secularization and inefficiency in propagation activities were problems demanding more serious attention.

Sōka Gakkai Enters Politics

Sōka Gakkai's doctrine of a national altar called for conversion of the masses and acquisition of seats in the national Diet so that an altar could be built at state expense at the Fuji headquarters temple of Taisekiji. Together with its forced conversion activities, Sōka Gakkai directed itself more and more to politics, setting forth a distinctive program for the unity of government and religion. In the general elections of April, 1955, Sōka Gakkai made its political debut by winning 53 seats in metropolitan and prefectural assemblies. After this, it expanded its election activities with the aid of the organization, and it steadily increased the number of seats it held in the House of Councillors as well as all levels of local assemblies. In the House of Councillors elections in the following year, it won three seats and obtained 3.5 percent of all votes cast; in the 1959 House of Councillors elections, it won six more seats and obtained 2,480,000 or 8.5 percent of all votes cast.

It was during the 1960 citizens' movement protesting the renewal of the U.S.-Japan Security Treaty that Sōka Gakkai solidified its position as a political force. It maintained a neutral position on the issue and increased its influence over the people. While established Buddhism was preoccupied by its own organizational reform and edification programs, Sōka Gakkai grew into such a large problem that it could no longer be ignored and had to be confronted directly.

In 1960, Ikeda Daisaku, on the basis of his work in the Youth Division, was installed as Sōka Gakkai's third president. Under Ikeda's leadership, in November of the next year Sōka Gakkai established the League of Fair Statesmen (Kōmei Seiji Remmei) as an auxiliary organization. The political advance of Sōka Gakkai up to this point had not followed a fixed political policy but had concentrated mainly on attacking established political parties through such slogans as "purification of politics," and "fair elections." Members were free to choose their political affiliation. However, with the formation of the Kōmei Seiji Remmei, it developed a political policy, thus adding substance to its political power. The three ideals it sought to pursue were: (1) concern for the conditions of the political world, (2) a political policy in which social prosperity is united with individual happiness, (3) political ideas based on the spirit of Nichiren. Initially, its basic political policy was: (1) opposition to nuclear weapons, (2) opposition to the revision of the Constitution, (3) fair elections and purification of politics, (4) establishing the independent character of the House of Councillors. The fourth item in 1963, following the formation of Sōka Gakkai's political policy, was revised to "establishing the democratic character of the Diet." As the keynote of their political policy they added (5) realization of the welfare of the masses. This fifth point was another way of wording Sōka Gakkai's belief in the ideal government of "unity of government and Buddhism" uniting individual happiness and social prosperity. The political philosophy of Sōka Gakkai skillfully captured public discontent and its distrust of government and sought to change actual conditions. Sōka Gakkai believed in the strengthening of state controls, the fulfillment of social guarantees, protection of the rights of medium- and small-scale business, and the cooperation of labor and capital. Its ideal was the realization of a modified capitalistic welfare state.

In the House of Councillors elections of July, 1962, all nine candidates who ran on the Kōmei Seiji Remmei ticket were elected. They received a total of 4,120,000 votes. The success of Sōka Gakkai's political advance was a great shock to other religious groups, and encouraged by the Liberal Democratic Party and Democratic Socialist Party, the political activities of established Buddhism, Shrine Shintō, and the new religions suddenly were intensified. In these elections, a candidate officially supported by Risshō Kōseikai and the Liberal Democratic Party was elected. In the next year's general local elections the Sōka Gakkai–Kōmei Seiji Remmei greatly increased their seats in all the prefectural and regional legislatures; they began with 55 seats, and after the elections occupied 1,102 seats.

Sōka Gakkai's social welfare program was expanded, and it set forth an unprecedented progressive program of new, selfless political ideals using such concepts as humanistic socialism, democracy based on Buddhist truth, and universalism. Socialism was criticized as not respecting humanism, and it was claimed that true democracy can be realized only if it is based on Buddhist truth (i.e., faith in Sōka Gakkai). Its universalism believed that if the world was considered as one nation, war would not occur. These were the extremely vague political ideas of Sōka Gakkai, closer to religious conviction than to political philosophy.

The Kōmei Seiji Remmei opened counseling centers throughout the country, and by efficiently organizing activities serving local needs, strengthened their political base. Within Sōka Gakkai, cultural activities through such educational means as a music appreciation organization for the masses, a general magazine called *Ushio* (The Tide), and the Oriental Research Institute were sponsored. Their activities among labor unions were improved, as were youth, student, and housewife organizations. Also, their overseas propagation sought total conversion of all Asia and the whole world. Starting with Okinawa as their first overseas advance, they proceeded to South Korea, Taiwan, and countries in Southeast

Asia, and North and South America. However, Sōka Gakkai was banned in Taiwan and Korea, for the reason that its aggressive nationalism would legitimize Japanese leadership in Asia.

Kōmeitō, A Centrist Party

In May, 1964, at Sōka Gakkai's general meeting, Ikeda first mentioned the plan to place its members in the House of Representatives and to form a religious political party. In November, the Kōmei Seiji Remmei was extensively reorganized and formed into the Kōmeitō, or Clean Government Party. By May of the same year, Sōka Gakkai had grown into one of Japan's foremost large religious organizations, with their publicly announced membership of 4,300,000 households, or more than 10,000,000 individuals. Kōmeitō thus became Japan's first actual religious political party, based on a program of unity of government and religion in the form of unity of government and Buddhism.

In the announcement of its formation as a political party, the Kōmeitō quoted Nichiren's phrase *risshō ankokuron* (the theory of establishment of righteousness and security of the country) and stated that it was based on the idea of the unity of government and Buddhism. Its objectives were outlined as: (1) permanent peace in the world through the unity of Buddhism and government, and universalism, (2) realization of welfare for the masses through humanistic socialism, (3) establishment of a political party for the masses through a Buddhistic democracy, (4) establishment of a parliamentary system of democratic government.

Kōmeitō and Sōka Gakkai were completely duplicate organizations. President Ikeda of Sōka Gakkai was the party's founder and a party leader. The religious prestige of Nichiren Shōshū/Sōka Gakkai penetrated Kōmeitō, and for Sōka Gakkai believers, propagation activities were difficult to distinguish from Kōmeitō's political activities. The intellectual class and the middle and lower ranks of the small business managerial class provided a stable leadership for the mass of believers from the urban lower salaried class of Sōka Gakkai. This structure came to determine Kōmeitō's political program to represent the political benefits of the middle and lower rank of the small business managerial class.

Kōmeitō claimed that it was a people's political party as well as a religious political party and cited the example of Christian political parties in Europe, arguing that the development of religious political parties in Japan was inevitable. However, the religious political parties in the capitalistic countries of Europe, even though they were based on Christian principles, were conservative, moderate political parties separate from a specific religious organization or religious authority, and in their political activities secularism had become the general trend. However, the structure of Kōmeitō, as a political party that relied on religious authority, is closer to the political groups derived from national religions seen in Islamic societies and the Buddhist countries of Southeast Asia.

In the House of Councillors election of July, 1965, the year after the formation of this party, it won 11 seats and won a total number of 5,090,000 votes, or 13.7 percent of all votes cast. Next, in the elections for the Tokyo Metropolitan Assembly, all 23 candidates were elected, and they became the third ranking party in the Metropolitan Assembly. In November, 1966, Kōmeitō did not run in the House of Representatives elections, and Ikeda advocated the "Wonderful Law of the Middle Path Principle" (myōhō no chū-dō shugi) which laid the doctrinal foundation of the welfare program for the masses. Middle-path politics was thus set forth as the basic course for Kōmeitō. From this time Sōka Gakkai consciously softened its aggressive proselytism and sought the support of the general public by cultural activities, and propagation was directed at the middle-class students, and the intellectual class.

In the general elections of January, 1967, Kōmeitō announced its candidacy in 32 electoral districts, mainly in the large cities, and won 25 seats. Kōmeitō/Sōka Gakkai became the fourth ranking party in the House of Representatives, and the third ranking party in the House of Councillors, and its relative political importance as the centrist political party holding the deciding vote between the Liberal Democratic and Socialist parties was thus increased. The Democratic Socialist and Communist parties and Kōmeitō became more prominent while the two major parties, the Liberal Democrats and Socialists, declined in power; the age of the multi-party system had arrived.

Sōka Gakkai's motives were to gain political power, and in opposition to this, the leaders of other religious groups increased their cooperation with the Liberal Democratic and Democratic Socialist parties. In December, 1965, a conference of religionists to discuss countermeasures to the situation was convened, gathering together the various Buddhist denominations, the Association of Shintō Shrines, the new religions, and Christians. In the following year, the Union of New Religious Organizations of Japan formed a political alliance and planned the mobilization of its affiliated organizations in the House of Representatives election. In the general local elections of April, 1967, Kōmeitō local assembly members increased to 107 members for metropolitan areas and prefectures, 1,291 members for cities and wards, 476 members for towns and villages—exceeding 1,800 seats.

In 1966, Kōmeitō opposed the small electoral district system, and after it formed a joint effort of opposition parties on the issue, it established itself as a centrist right-wing opposition party. With regard to the subject of the 1970 Security Treaty renewal, it proposed a gradual dissolution of the Security Treaty. But its political policy was characteristic of a petit bourgeois party, wavering between Right and Left.

In the House of Councillors election of July, 1968, nine Kōmeitō members were elected from the national constituency, and four from the prefectural constituencies (Tokyo, Aichi, Osaka, and Hyōgo). Nationwide their votes increased to more than 6,650,000, or 15.4 percent of the total vote. In addition to establishing its position as the centrist political party, Kōmeitō increased its support outside of Sōka Gakkai and competed with the Democratic Socialist Party. It aimed at becoming the second ranking opposition party and launched diverse activities, such as strengthening political publicity, advocating the formation of unions, and sponsoring cultural activities.

In this process Kōmeitō gradually minimized its religious character and began to assume the posture of a political party free of the framework of a religious political party. Sōka Gakkai, which developed rapidly in its political advance based on a distinctive principle of the unity of government and religion, became the most important focus of religious problems in the 1960s. However, this anachronistic policy of unity of government and religion, together with the movement to restore State Shintō, which aimed at a revival of the imperial system of the unity of government and religion, threatened the Japanese Constitution's basic principles of freedom of religion, and separation of government and religion.

15. Religion in Japan Today

In the decade or so from the mid-1960s, Japanese society experienced major social change. Japanese capitalism continued to grow at a rapid rate and penetrated the markets of Southeast Asia and then throughout the world. Eventually, the high quality and low prices of Japanese products threatened European and American industries. However, in the 1970s the successive oil crises rocked the economic world, the growth of the Japanese economy suddenly stagnated, and society as a whole suffered from inflation. Japan entered a period of slow economic growth, and a new international environment emerged with the aggravation of relations between China and the Soviet Union, the conclusion of the Vietnam War, and the Japanese and American restoration of relations with China. To cope with this situation, Japan strengthened military and economic ties with South Korea and the United States, and within Japan the trend toward reactionary politics has continued.

The Revival of the Emperor System

The various religions of Japan reflected these changing internal and external conditions and intensified their social and political activities. In October, 1968, the government sponsored the Meiji Centennial celebration honoring the one hundredth anniversary of the Meiji Restoration of 1868. This was analogous to directly linking the contemporary Japanese state of popular sovereignty with the former Japanese empire of imperial sovereignty, and served to strengthen the move to reinstate the earlier imperial state and excuse its aggressive wars. Taking advantage of this opportunity,

157

the movement to restore State Shintō displayed an unprecedented upsurge.

In 1973, the ritual rebuilding of Ise Shrine took place, and Princess Takatsukasa Kazuko, the third daughter of the emperor, served as the temporary chief priestess of Ise. The next year, the emperor and empress made a pilgrimage to Ise Shrine and on that occasion they revived the ritual of *kenji dōza*. This is a ritual performed on the occasion of the emperor's travels, when two of the three sacred regalia of the imperial throne, the sword and jewel, accompanied the emperor; this ritual had been abolished after World War II.

In November, 1976, ceremonies honoring the fiftieth anniversary of the emperor's rule were conducted on a grand scale, and the movement to restore the imperial system reached a new stage. In August, 1977, at a summer resort in Nasu, Tochigi Prefecture, the emperor made a public statement in which he denied that in 1946 he had actually disclaimed his divine character and proclaimed his human character. On February 11, 1978, National Foundation Day, for the first time the government encouraged popular celebration rites, and once more made clear its position on commemorating the origin of the imperial state. The same year conservative forces sought legislation on the tradition of maintaining an era name for the duration of an emperor's reign. This problem of era names became the focus of much political conflict.

During this period the movement for state administration of Yasukuni Shrine intensified. In June, 1969, the Liberal Democratic Party presented the Yasukuni Shrine Bill to the Diet. This bill, whose import was to consider the Yasukuni Shrine as a non-religious special foundation and to place it under the jurisdiction of the prime minister, was an open violation of the Constitution. The driving force behind the movement, religious groups, such as the Association of Shintō Shrines, Seichō no Ie, and Bussho Gonenkai, and also the Survivors' Association, the Goyū Remmei, and right-wing groups, participated in an active nationwide movement for the bill. In opposition to this, peace movements within various religions—Christians; within the new religions, Risshō Kōseikai, Perfect Liberty, and Myōchikai; and within established Buddhist sects, the Jōdo Shinshū Honganji sect and the Shinshū Ōtani sect—were a broad democractic force which developed into a deep-rooted opposition movement. They held that state administration of Yasukuni Shrine would be a revival of State Shintō and would open the door to the reemergence of Japanese militarism. This bill was presented to the Diet six times before June, 1974, and during this period faced such opposition from citizens at all levels that the bill failed.

In February, 1975, the Liberal Democratic Party made public the concept of the so-called Memorial Respect Proposal and immediately expressed its intention of legislating formal visits to Yasukuni Shrine by such figures as the emperor and prime minister. Formal visits by the emperor and prime minister would mean that Yasukuni Shrine, which is a religious juridical person, is considered to have a national or public status. This constituted a frontal attack on the basic principle of separation of religion and state as determined by the Constitution. In the same year on August 15th, the anniversary of Japan's surrender in World War II, Prime Minister Miki Takeo visited Yasukuni Shrine, the first postwar visit for a prime minister; thereafter it became customary for these de facto official visits by the prime minister to be made. In June, 1976, an association was formed in honor of the souls of the war dead, with the purpose of developing a nationwide people's movement for legislation on official visits to Yasukuni Shrine, and many conservative religious leaders lent their names in support of this cause

In 1965, in the city of Tsu, Mie Prefecture, city officials used public funds to perform a Shrine Shintō form of ritual called *jichin* (invoking *kami* to bless a building site). A communist member of the Tsu city council brought suit, charging that this was a violation of the Constitution. In court the argument was whether a Shrine Shintō form of *jichin* ritual was a religious act or a common custom. In 1971, the Nagoya High Court ruled that the use of Tsu public funds was a violation of the Constitution. The city of Tsu appealed, and in July, 1977, the Supreme Court laid down its decision that the city of Tsu's action had been constitutional, thus supporting the theory of the nonreligious character of shrines, which in turn was the basis for the argument to restore State Shintō.

The movement to restore State Shintō is based on the religious consciousness of the majority of citizens, who accept Shrine Shintō as a public religion, as they did in prewar times. In opposition to this infringement on the principle of the separation of state and religion a counter-movement has developed momentum. This opposition movement has exposed the close connection between shrines and regional public organizations as well as citizens' groups throughout the country.

In 1973, the widow of an official of the Self-Defense Force, who had died while on duty in an automobile accident, sued the state for enshrining her husband in a *gokoku jinja* of Yamaguchi Prefecture. Her litigation claimed that this was a violation of freedom of religion by the state (that is, the Self-Defense Force), because it was an infringement on the basis principle of the separation of state and religion. In the trial the militaristic character of the *gokoku jinja* and Yasukuni Shrine (which were strong supporters of State Shintō) became evident, and the unconstitutional character of state administration of Yasukuni Shrine became patently clear.

Internal Conflict Within the Shinshū Ōtani Sect

Under the conditions of rapid growth, the major sects of established Buddhism strengthened ties between parishioners and temples, putting their energy into educational activities. Within the Pure Land sects an increase in membership was sought through the *otetsugi* movement; the Tendai sects developed the *ichigu o terasu* movement, a social welfare program to help the needy. In one of the powerful sects, the Jōdo Shinshū Honganji sect, a movement of the parishioners' association, which had begun in 1962, resulted in the gradual reform of the character of the religious body. In 1962, there began within the Shinshū Ōtani sect the Dōbōkai (Brotherhood) Movement, which had as its goal the establishment of a new doctrine and the reform of the religious body. However, as the movement grew, a struggle intensified between the conservative faction, which had on its side the Abbot Ōtani Kōchō (1903–), and the reform faction.

The Dōbōkai Movement was heir to the thought of Kiyozawa Manshi (1863–1903) that urged the modernization of the religious body by revolutionizing the traditional reliance on ties between temples and families. It raised the concept of developing a new religious body in terms of brotherhood (dōbō) based on small groups of believers and their individual faith. In the 1970s, the reform faction became the majority in the sect's deliberative body.

The conservative faction gradually disposed of the religious body's capital, claiming that this action was taken in defense of the sect, and in opposition to the advance of the reform faction which threatened the position of the abbot who combined the three offices of abbot, superintendent priest, and chief priest of the main temple, Honganji. In 1978, the reform faction rejected the Ōtani superintendent priest and selected a new superintendent priest. The abbot retaliated by rejecting the appointment of the sect's director of religious affairs and the superintendent priest of the reform faction, and declared the independence of Higashi Honganji from the religious body. The reform faction then sued the abbot and his followers concerning their disposal of the sect's finances.

Thus the dispute over Higashi Honganji fell into a quagmire. But the premodern character of this religious body, with its view of the absolute power of the abbot of the Ōtani family (in whose veins flowed the blood of the founder Shinran), was seriously shaken. In most of the sects of established Buddhism, because the movement to democratize religious bodies during the postwar Occupation had failed, their semi-feudal character was preserved, and the intensification of the reform movement in the Shinshū Ōtani sect was a great shock to other Buddhist sects.

Dispute in the United Church of Christ

In 1967, the president of the United Church of Christ in Japan (Nihon Kirisuto Kyōdan), Suzuki Masahisa (1912–69), as representative of this religious body, made a public confession of the church's cooperation in the war effort. This religious body, out of all Japanese religions, thus became the first to voluntarily undergo self-criticism for its responsibility in an aggressive war.

This religious body, in conjunction with Catholics, set up a Christian exhibit at the World Exposition held in Osaka in 1970. Some of the members and clergy of the church felt that participation in the World Exposition was cooperating with the revival of militarism and imperialism that the government was promoting, and this provoked a strong opposition movement. At this juncture, criticism against the leadership of the church increased, and there were campus disturbances at Tokyo Union Theological Seminary. In 1972, the Methodist-affiliated Aoyama Gakuin University and the Baptist-affiliated Kantō Gakuin University abolished their theology faculties, giving as their reason the rationalization of school administration. The dispute of the United Church of Christ in Japan was especially strong in Tokyo and Osaka, such that they were unable to hold formal general assemblies until the latter half of the 1970s.

Trends in the New Religions

Due to rapid economic growth, the major new religions greeted a period of stability and were able to concentrate on organizational consolidation and internal structure. The federation of new religions, known as the Shin Nihon Shūkyōdantai Rengōkai (Union of New Religious Organizations of Japan), under the leadership of Risshō Kōseikai and Perfect Liberty raised the slogans of "religious cooperation, freedom of religion, separation of religion and state, and a faith for all people." This federation opposed state administration of Yasukuni Shrine and developed a wide opposition movement. In 1969, Risshō Kōseikai promoted their religious body by initiating a movement to create a happy society and developed close regional ties; through cooperation with other organizations they proceeded to enlarge and firmly establish their institutional strength. In 1965, President Niwano Nikkyō was the only Japanese religious leader invited to the Second Vatican Council as an observer. On this occasion, in line with the policy of religious cooperation put forth by the Vatican, President Niwano launched an international religious peace movement.

In October, 1970, the World Conference on Religion and Peace (Sekai Shūkyōsha Heiwa Kaigi) was convened at Kyoto, with Risshō Kōseikai as the leading force. Representatives from nine countries participated, discussing the themes of demilitarization, development, and human rights. As a result of this conference, in

1972, the Japanese Committee of the World Conference on Religion and Peace was formed, and Risshō Kōseikai once more became the main force, developing the religion and peace movement both domestically and internationally.

Reiyūkai in 1964 built a sanctuary called Mirokuzan at Izu in Shizuoka Prefecture and in their doctrine adopted faith in Miroku as the savior of the Buddhist age of decadence. In 1971, President Kotani Kimi passed away and Kubo Tsugunari (1936–) was installed as president. President Kubo launched his "inner trip" movement (in the sense of turning inward toward the human heart), and received a good response from the younger generation. In 1975, they completed the Buddha Hall (Shakaden) at their headquarters, demonstrating the resurgence of Reiyūkai's institutional strength.

Seichō no Ie in 1964 created the Seichō no Ie Political Alliance (Seichō no Ie Seiji Rengō), and, joining hands with conservative forces, assumed a positive posture concerning politics. Within Seichō no Ie activities favoring direct rule by the emperor and the restoration of State Shintō increased. In 1978, they completed the large Sacred Place of Sumiyoshi Hongū (Sumiyoshi Main Shrine) in Nagasaki Prefecture.

Sekai Kyūsei-kyō in the early 1970s unified its religious body, but in the process several of its powerful branches became independent. Since then, this new religion has become a conservative organization, supporting state administration of Yasukuni Shrine and withdrawing from the Union of New Religious Organizations of Japan.

Bussho Gonenkai, too, which had made large contributions to the rebuilding of Ise Shrine, giving as its reason the Yasukuni problem, withdrew from the Union of New Religious Organizations of Japan.

In 1972, the Korean new religion Unification Church (known in Japan as Sekai Kirisuto Tōitsu Shinrei Kyōkai, literally Holy Spirit Association for Unification of World Christianity) began propagation work in Japan. This religion is derived from Christianity and had its beginnings in Seoul, Korea, where it was founded by Moon Sun Myung in 1954. The doctrine of this religion teaches that the founder Moon is the messiah or savior of the Second Coming (of Christ), Korea is a divine country, and socialist countries are viewed with enmity as satanic countries. In the 1970s, this religion's social action organization, Genri Kenkyūkai (Society for the Study of the Divine Principle), expanded remarkably within many universities, and also stepped up its activities in political groups and its Federation for International Victory over Communism (Kokusai Shōkyō Rengō). The development of Unification Church became a social problem. Young members were brainwashed and abandoned their families, provoking an opposition movement created by the parents of such followers. Because this religion called itself a Christian movement, it came under increasing attack from other Christian groups.

Changes in Sōka Gakkai

Sōka Gakkai, which has grown into Japan's largest religious force, entered a period of stability from the mid-1960s. At the end of 1969, the leaders of Sōka Gakkai and Kōmeitō were exposed for their suppression of the publication of a series of books criticizing Sōka Gakkai, and public criticism mounted against Sōka Gakkai's undemocratic character. In May, 1970, President Ikeda Daisaku announced the separation of Kōmeitō and Sōka Gakkai, and attempted to appease public opinion. Kōmeitō leaders were removed from their positions in Sōka Gakkai and religious terminology was deleted from the party platform and bylaws. Within Sōka Gakkai, in order to settle the internal disorder caused by this separation, a reform of both doctrine and organization was sought, and in terms of activities, emphasis was shifted to such spheres as education, the arts, international relations, and the peace movement. But it was not before long that the former unity of Sōka Gakkai with Kōmeitō was in reality restored.

In 1972, the huge modern building Shōhondō was completed at Taisekiji, Nichiren Shōshū headquarters; within Sōka Gakkai it was considered that this was the actual altar of "true teaching" (*hommon*). Out of the necessity of increasing Kōmeitō's party strength, Sōka Gakkai rejected its earlier stated intention of creating a national altar, claiming that with the construction of the Shōhondō, the objective of conversion of the entire world (*kōsen rufu*) as an eternal goal of faith had already been achieved. This change in doctrine was met with opposition and criticism from Nichiren Shōshū lay groups, such as Myōshinkō.

In December, 1974, Sōka Gakkai secretly made a ten-year pact with the Japan Communist Party to act together for such purposes as anti-fascism. This pact was made public in July, 1975, and came as a shock to the entire society. The Communist Party claimed that it was an agreement to fight together as a united front but Sōka Gakkai countered this interpretation by saying that the pact was no more than mutual consent to coexist. Because of this difference of interpretation on both sides, the pact shortly became a dead letter. Kōmeitō opposed the pact and resumed its anti-communist stand. In 1978, Kōmeitō crossed sides by approving the Security Treaty, and by switching from its moderate progressive viewpoint of cooperating with the Socialist and Democratic Socialist parties to the conservative moderate alliance linked with the Liberal Democratic and Democratic Socialist parties, Kōmeitō began to support conservative policies.

Religion and Political Change

In 1974, the conservative leaders of both the established and new religions participated in the formation of Nihon o Mamoru Kai, an association whose aim was to defend Japan; they supported the political reactionaries who were hostile to democracy. In 1970, the ties between some powerful religious bodies, on the one hand, and the Liberal Democratic and the Democratic Socialist parties, on the other hand, became even stronger. During elections the powerful religious bodies became a large and reliable pool of voters for political parties. The leaders of religious bodies flaunted their religious authority by specifically telling their believers whom to vote for. Powerful religious bodies—Seichō no Ie, Reiyū-kai, Bussho Gonenkai, Jinja Honchō, and Sekai Kyūsei-kyō, and members of the Union of New Religious Organizations, such as Risshō Kōseikai, Perfect Liberty, and Myōchikai—all became a prominent base for the Liberal Democratic Party. (Sekai Kyūsei-kyō also worked with the Democratic Socialist Party.)

Coupled with the expansion of such close cooperation between religious bodies and political parties, and including the existence of Kōmeitō which had Sōka Gakkai as its largest supporting organization, the direct influence that religious organizations exerted on political activities steadily increased. In 1977, the Liberal Democratic Party, with the intention of concentrating support from religious organizations, formed a group for the study of religion and politics (Shūkyō Seiji Kenkyū Kai). This group, which was under the strong influence of Seichō no Ie, intended to mobilize the established and new religious organizations for reactionary politics, such as the strengthening of the emperor system.

In opposition to this general trend in the religious world that cooperated in reactionary politics, there were progressive clergy and members of various religions who opposed state administration of Yasukuni Shrine. These forces concentrated their strength in the Japanese Religionists Council for Peace (Nihon Shūkyōsha Heiwa Kyōgikai) and the peace organizations within various religions; they also volunteered their help in such causes as the protection of freedom of religion, the banning of nuclear weapons, and aid to atomic bomb victims, oppostion to the Vietnam War, and the establishment of a Sino-Japanese friendship treaty.

In 1969, the first World Federation of Religions for the Promotion of Peace Conference (Sekai Rempō Heiwa Sokushin Shūkyōsha Taikai) was held at Minobu, Yamanashi Prefecture, and the leaders of established Buddhism, Ōmoto-kyō, and others who participated passed a resolution favoring the promotion of a world federation. In Tokyo in 1972, a world assembly of religions for peace and justice in Indochina was held with religious representatives from socialist countries participating; it passed a resolution of solidarity with the Democratic Republic of Vietnam and opposition to the Vietnam War.

In Japanese society during the 1970s, with the increasing trend toward reactionary politics, the close relationship between religion and politics has become patently clear, such that even the restoration of State Shintō by the government was publicly promoted. The basic democratic principles of freedom of religion and separation of state and religion as specified by the Constitution are faced with a serious threat today.

In a democratic society, religion should be separated from politics; its principal role in helping to attain inner salvation should be the private affair of citizens, and cooperation and mutual understanding among the various religions should be promoted. The age when political reform and national independence were brought about by religion, and expressed through distorted religious ideology at long last is becoming a relic of the past.

The clergy and members of contemporary Japan's various religions have the social responsibility to protect the freedom of religion and can contribute to the peace and prosperity of the people. The people have the right to reject both state exploitation of religion, and religious control of the state, and public criticism against religions that curry favor with the state and serve reactionary purposes should be openly made. Indeed, history demonstrates how in the past one hundred years Japanese society has sought freedom of religion, an indispensable condition for religions to grow freely without interference and to allow their rich traditions to thrive in a changing society.

Appendix I. Major Buddhist, Shintō, and Christian Organizations

Lineage	Religious Body	Headquarters	Year of Founding*	Adherents (in thousands)†
Buddhist (Nara sects)	Hossō Shū	Nara	653	594
	Kegon Shū	Nara	740	44
	Risshū	Nara	759	26
	Shingon Risshū	Nara	1236	475
(Tendai sects)	Tendai Shū	Ōtsu, Shiga Pref.	805	610
	Tendai Shinseishū	Ōtsu, Shiga Pref.	1485	64
	Shugen Shū	Odawara, Kanagawa Pref.	(1946)	98
	Wa Shū	Tennōji-ku, Osaka	1949	2,221
(Shingon sects)	Kōyasan Shingonshū	Kōya, Wakayama Pref.	861	4,277
	Shingonshū Daigoha	Fushimi-ku, Kyoto	(1900)	341
	Shingonshū Buzanha	Bunkyō-ku, Tokyo	1587	1,189
	Shingonshū Chizanha	Higashiyama-ku, Kyoto	1598	1,529
(Pure Land sects)	Jōdo Shū	Higashiyama-ku, Kyoto	1175	5,967
	Jōdo Shinshū Honganjiha	Shimogyō-ku, Kyoto	1224	6,907
	Shinshū Ōtaniha	Shimogyō-ku, Kyoto	1224	6,150
	Shinshū Takadaha	Tsu, Mie Pref.	(1877)	269
	Jishū	Fujisawa, Kanagawa Pref.	1273	335
(Zen sects)	Sōtō Shū	Minato-ku, Tokyo	1227	7,532
	Rinzaishū Myōshinjiha	Ukyō-ku, Kyoto	1336	693
	Rinzaishū Kenchōjiha	Kamakura, Kanagawa Pref.	1446	200

Rinzaishū Hōkōjiha	Inasa, Shizuoka Pref.	(1903)	69
Ōbaku Shū	Uji, Kyoto	1654	321
(Nichiren sects)			
Nichiren Shū	Ōta-ku, Tokyo	1253	2,281
Nichiren Shōshū	Fujinomiya, Shizuoka Pref.	1288	16,362‡
Hokkeshū (Hommonryū)	Toshima-ku, Tokyo	(1941)	561
Nichirenshū Fujufuseha	Mitsu, Okayama Pref.	1595	28
Shintō			
Jinja Honchō	Shibuya-ku, Tokyo	(1946)	61,630
Jinja Honkyō	Yamashina-ku, Kyoto	(1946)	809
Christian			
Katorikku Chūō Kyōgikai (Catholic Church in Japan)	Chiyoda-ku, Tokyo	1549	350
Nihon Harisutosu Seikyō-kai Kyōdan (Holy Orthodox Church in Japan)	Chiyoda-ku, Tokyo	1861	10
Nihon Kirisuto Kyōdan (United Church of Christ in Japan)	Shinjuku-ku, Tokyo	(1941)	135
Nihon Seikōkai (Anglican Episcopal Church of Japan)	Shibuya-ku, Tokyo	1859	55

* Parentheses around the year of founding indicate the official organization of the religious body.
† Numbers of adherents obtained from the figures supplied by religious bodies for the *Shūkyō Nenkan* (1978), ed. Agency for Cultural Affairs, Ministry of Education, Science and Culture.
‡ Nichiren Shōshū figures include adherents to Sōka Gakkai.

Appendix II. Major New Religions

Lineage	Religious Body	Headquarters	Year of Founding	Adherents (in thousands)*
Buddhism	Nyorai-kyō	Atsuta-ku, Nagoya	1802	34
Shintō	Kurozumi-kyō	Okayama	1814	381
Other	Tenri-kyō	Tenri, Nara Pref.	1838	2,485
Shintō	Misogi-kyō	Taitō-ku, Tokyo	1840	125
Shintō	Shinri-kyō	Kokura Minami-ku, Kita Kyūshū	1843	275
Buddhism	Hommon Butsuryūshū	Kamigyō-ku, Kyoto	1857	510
Shintō	Konkō-kyō	Konkō, Okayama Pref.	1859	490
Shintō	Izumo Ōyashiro-kyō	Taisha, Shimane Pref.	1873	1,050
Shintō	Ontake-kyō	Nara	1873	733
Shintō	Maruyama-kyō	Tama-ku, Kawasaki	1873	3
Shintō	Ōmoto-kyō	Kameoka, Kyoto	1892	162
Shintō	Hommichi	Takaishi, Osaka	1913	294
Buddhism	Kokuchūkai	Edogawa-ku, Tokyo	1914	23
Buddhism	Nihonzan Myōhōji	Shibuya-ku, Tokyo	1917	1
Other	Ennō-kyō	Sannan, Hyōgo Pref.	1919	287
Buddhism	Reiyūkai	Minato-ku, Tokyo	1923	2,700
Other	Perfect Liberty (PL) Kyōdan	Tondabayashi, Osaka	1924	2,646
Buddhism	Nempō Shinkyō	Tsurumi-ku, Osaka	1925	854
Buddhism	Gedatsukai	Shinjuku, Tokyo	1929	455
Other	Seichō no Ie	Shibuya-ku, Tokyo	1930	3,096

Buddhism	Sōka Gakkai	Shinjuku-ku, Tokyo	1930	16,539
Other	Sekai Kyūsei-kyō	Atami, Shizuoka Pref.	1934	790
Buddhism	Kōdō Kyōdan	Kanagawa-ku, Yokohama	1935	418
Buddhism	Risshō Kōseikai	Suginami-ku, Tokyo	1938	4,742
Other	Tenshō Kōtai Jingū-kyō	Tabuse, Yamaguchi Pref.	1945	400
Other	Zenrinkai	Tsukushino, Fukuoka Pref.	1947	578
Buddhism	Shinnyoen	Tachikawa, Tokyo	1948	455
Shintō	Ananai-kyō	Shimizu, Shizuoka Pref.	1949	218
Buddhism	Myōchikai	Shibuya-ku, Tokyo	1950	679
Buddhism	Bussho Gonenkai	Minato-ku, Tokyo	1950	1,474
Buddhism	Saijō Inari-kyō	Okayama	1951	286

* Number of adherents obtained from figures supplied by religious bodies for the *Shūkyō Nenkan* (1978), ed. Agency for Cultural Affairs, Ministry of Education, Science and Culture.

Selected Bibliography

Abe, Yoshiya. "Religious Freedom under the Meiji Constitution," *Contemporary Religions in Japan* IX (1968): 268–338; a book-length work serialized in the next five issues of this journal.

Anesaki, Masaharu. *History of Japanese Religion*. 1930. Reprint. Rutland, Vermont: Charles E. Tuttle Co., 1963.

Beasley, W. G. *The Meiji Restoration*. Stanford: Stanford University Press, 1972.

Bellah, Robert N. *Tokugawa Religion*. 1957. Reprint. Boston: Beacon Press, 1970.

Brown, Delmer M. *Nationalism in Japan. An Introductory Historical Analysis*. Berkeley and Los Angeles: University of California Press, 1955.

Butow, Robert J. C. *Tojo and the Coming of the War*. Princeton: Princeton University Press, 1961.

Byas, Hugh. *Government by Assassination*. New York: Alfred A. Knopf, 1942.

Cary, Otis. *A History of Christianity in Japan*. 2 vols. 1909. Reprint. St. Clair Shores, Michigan: Scholarly Press, 1970.

Creemers, Wilhelmus H. M. *Shrine Shinto After World War II*. Leiden: E. J. Brill, 1968.

Davis, Winston Bradley. *Dojo: Exorcism and Miracles in Modern Japan*. Stanford: Stanford University Press, forthcoming.

———. *Toward Modernity: A Developmental Typology of Popular Religious Affiliations in Japan*. Ithaca, N.Y.: Cornell China-Japan Program, 1977.

Dore, R. P. *City Life in Japan. A Study of a Tokyo Ward*. Berkeley and Los Angeles: University of California Press, 1958.

Drummond, Richard H. *A History of Christianity in Japan*. Grand Rapids, Mich.: William B. Eerdmans Publishing Co., 1971.

Duus, Peter. *Feudalism in Japan*. 2d ed. New York: Alfred A. Knopf, 1976.

Earhart, H. Byron. *Japanese Religion: Unity and Diversity*. 3d ed. Belmont, California: Wadsworth Publishing Co., forthcoming.

————. *The New Religions of Japan. A Bibliography of Western-Language Materials*. 2d ed. Boston: G. K. Hall & Co., forthcoming.

Earl, David Magarey. *Emperor and Nation in Japan. Political Thinkers of the Tokugawa Period*. Seattle: University of Washington Press, 1964.

Fairbank, John K.; Reischauer, Edwin O.; and Craig, Albert M. *East Asia: The Modern Transformation*. Boston: Houghton Mifflin Company, 1965.

Frager, Robert and Rohlen, Thomas P. "The Future of a Tradition: Japanese Spirit in the 1980s." In *Japan: The Paradox of Progress*, edited by Lewis Austin, pp. 255–78. New Haven: Yale University Press, 1976.

Fridell, Wilbur M. *Japanese Shrine Mergers 1906–12. State Shinto Moves to the Grassroots*. Tokyo: Sophia University, 1973.

Fujiwara, Hirotatsu. *I Denounce Soka Gakkai*. Translated by Worth C. Grant. Tokyo: Nishin Hodo Co., 1970.

Gauntlett, John Owen, trans. *Kokutai no Hongi: Cardinal Principles of the National Entity of Japan*. Edited by Robert King Hall. Cambridge: Harvard University Press, 1949.

Hall, John Whitney. *Japanese History. New Dimensions of Approach and Understanding*. 2d ed. Washington, D.C.: American Historical Association, 1966.

————. "A Monarch for Modern Japan." In *Political Development in Modern Japan*, edited by Robert E. Ward, pp. 11–64. Princeton: Princeton University Press, 1968.

Hall, Robert King. *Shushin: The Ethics of a Defeated Nation*. New York: Columbia University, 1949.

Halliday, Jon, and McCormack, Gavin. *Japanese Imperialism Today: Co-Prosperity in Greater East Asia*. Harmondsworth: Penguin Books, 1973.

Haraguchi, Torao et al. *The Status System and Social Organization of Satsuma. A Translation of the* Shumon Tefuda Aratame Jomoku. Honolulu: University Press of Hawaii, 1976.

Holtom, Daniel C. *Modern Japan and Shinto Nationalism. A Study of*

Present-day Trends in Japanese Religions. Rev. ed. 1947. Reprint.
New York: Paragon Reprint Corp., 1963.

————. *The National Faith of Japan. A Study in Modern Shinto*.
1938. Reprint. New York: Paragon Reprint Corp., 1965.

Hori, Ichiro. *Folk Religion in Japan. Continuity and Change*. Edited by
Joseph M. Kitagawa and Alan L. Miller. Chicago: University
of Chicago Press, 1968.

————, ed. *Japanese Religion*. Translated by Yoshiya Abe and
David Reid. Tokyo and Palo Alto: Kodansha International,
1972.

Iglehart, Charles W. *A Century of Protestant Christianity in Japan*.
Rutland, Vermont: Charles E. Tuttle Co., 1958.

Ikado, Fujio. "Trend and Problems of New Religions: Religion in
Urban Society." In *The Sociology of Japanese Religion,* edited by
Kiyoma Morioka and William H. Newell, pp. 101–17. Leiden:
E. J. Brill, 1968.

Inoguchi, Rikihei; and Nakajima, Tadashi; with Pineau, Roger.
The Divine Wind. Japan's Kamikaze Force in World War II. New
York: Bantam Books, 1960.

Institute for Japanese Culture and Classics, Kokugakuin University. *Proceedings, The Second International Conference for Shinto
Studies*. Tokyo: Kokugakuin University, 1968.

Jansen, Marius B., ed. *Changing Japanese Attitudes Toward Modernization*. Princeton: Princeton University Press, 1965.

Johnston, Gilbert L. "Kiyozawa Manshi: A Shinshu Buddhist
View of Stoic Self-Reliance." *Japanese Religions* IV (1966): 31–44.

Kanamori, Tokujiro et al. *Religion and State in Japan: A Discussion
of Religion and State in Relation to the Constitution*. Bulletin No. 7.
Tokyo: International Institute for the Study of Religions, 1959.

Kishimoto, Hideo, ed. *Japanese Religion in the Meiji Era*. Translated
by John F. Howes. Tokyo: Obunsha, 1956.

Kitagawa, Joseph M. *Religion in Japanese History*. New York:
Columbia University Press, 1966.

————. "The Religions of Japan." In *A Reader's Guide to the Great
Religions,* 2d ed., edited by Charles J. Adams, pp. 247–82. New
York: Free Press, 1977.

Kiyota, Minoru. "Buddhism in Postwar Japan. A Critical Survey," *Monumenta Nipponica* XXIV (1969): 113–36.

Lebra, Joyce C. *Japan's Greater East Asia Co-Prosperity Sphere in World War II.* Kuala Lumpur: Oxford University Press, 1975.

Lockwood, William W. *The Economic Development of Japan: Growth and Structural Change.* Expanded ed. Princeton: Princeton University Press, 1968.

McFarland, H. Neill. *The Rush Hour of the Gods. A Study of the New Religious Movements in Japan.* New York: Macmillan Company, 1967.

Mitchell, Richard H. *Thought Control in Prewar Japan.* Ithaca, N.Y.: Cornell University Press, 1976.

Morioka, Kiyomi. *Religion in Changing Japanese Society.* Tokyo: University of Tokyo Press, 1975.

Morioka, Kiyomi and Newell, William H., eds. *The Sociology of Japanese Religion.* Leiden: E. J. Brill, 1968.

Morris, Ivan. *Nationalism and the Right Wing in Japan: A Study of Postwar Trends.* London: Oxford University Press, 1960.

Muraoka, Tsunetsugu. *Studies in Shinto Thought.* Translated by Delmer M. Brown and James T. Araki. Tokyo: Ministry of Education, 1964.

Najita, Tetsuo. *Japan.* Englewood Cliffs, N.J.: Prentice-Hall, 1974.

Nakane, Chie. *Japanese Society.* Berkeley and Los Angeles: University of California Press, 1972.

Norbeck, Edward. *Religion and Society in Modern Japan: Continuity and Change.* Houston: Tourmaline Press, 1970.

Organizing Committee for Tokyo Meeting of CISR. *Proceedings of Tokyo Meeting of the International Conference on Sociology of Religion 1978.* Tokyo: Organizing Committee for Tokyo Meeting of CISR 1978, 1978.

Plath, David W. "The Fate of Utopia: Adaptive Tactics in Four Japanese Groups." *American Anthropologist* LXVIII (1966): 1152–62.

Scheiner, Irwin. *Christian Converts and Social Protest in Meiji Japan.* Berkeley and Los Angeles: University of California Press, 1970.

Shively, Donald H., ed. *Tradition and Modernization in Japanese Culture.* Princeton: Princeton University Press, 1971.

Smith, Robert J. *Kurusu: The Price of Progress in a Japanese Village 1951–1975.* Stanford: Stanford University Press, 1978.

Smith, Thomas C. *The Agrarian Origins of Modern Japan.* Stanford: Stanford University Press, 1959.

Smith, Warren W., Jr. *Confucianism in Modern Japan. A Study of*

Conservatism in Japanese Intellectual History. 2d ed. Tokyo: Hokuseido Press, 1973.

Storry, Richard. *The Double Patriots. A Study of Japanese Nationalism.* London: Chatto and Windus, 1957.

Sugihara, Yoshie, and Plath, David W. *Sensei and His People. The Building of a Japanese Commune.* Berkeley and Los Angeles: University of California Press, 1969.

Sunoo, Harold Hakwon. *Japanese Militarism: Past and Present.* Chicago: Nelson-Hall, 1975.

Tsukamoto, Zenryu. "Japanese and Chinese Buddhism." In *Religions and the Promise of the Twentieth Century,* edited by Guy S. Metraux and Francois Crouzet, pp. 229–44. New York: New American Library, 1965.

Tsunoda, Ryusaku et al. *Sources of Japanese Tradition.* New York: Columbia University Press, 1958.

Union of the New Religious Organizations in Japan, Research Office, ed. "Reminiscences of Religion in Postwar Japan." *Contemporary Religions in Japan* VI (1965): 111–203; a book-length work serialized in the next five issues of this journal.

Van Hecken, Joseph L. *The Catholic Church in Japan Since 1859.* Translated by John Van Hoydonck. Tokyo: Enderle Bookstore, 1963.

Vogel, Ezra F. *Japan's New Middle Class: The Salary Man and His Family in a Tokyo Suburb.* 2d ed. Berkeley and Los Angeles: University of California Press, 1971.

Ward, Robert E. *Japan's Political System.* 2d ed. Englewood Cliffs, N.J.: Prentice-Hall, 1978.

Watanabe, Shoko. *Japanese Buddhism—A Critical Appraisal.* Translated by Alfred Bloom. Tokyo: Kokusai Bunka Shinkokai, 1964.

White, James W. *The Sokagakkai and Mass Society.* Stanford: Stanford University Press, 1970.

Wilson, George M. *Radical Nationalist in Japan: Kita Ikki 1883–1937.* Cambridge: Harvard University Press, 1969.

Woodard, William P. *The Allied Occupation of Japan 1945–1952 and Japanese Religions.* Leiden: E. J. Brill, 1972.

———. "Study on Religious Juridical Persons Law, Text of the Law No. 126 of 1951." *Contemporary Japan* XXV (1958): 418–70; a book-length work serialized in the next three issues of this journal.

Index

agrarian land reform, 122–23
agriculture, 4, 7, 72, 96, 140
  See also agrarian land reform
All-Japan Buddhist Association (Zen Nihon Bukkyō Kai), 126, 130
All-Japan Conference of Buddhists (Zen Nihon Bukkyōtō Kyōkai), 126
Amaterasu Ōmikami, 13, 19, 21, 23, 41, 73, 86–87, 88, 98–99, 104, 110 112, 139
American Baptist Church, 36
American Congregational Church, 38–39, 48
American Episcopal Church, 36
American Presbyterian Church, 36–38
Amida, 26, 144
anarchists, 55, 57, 61
ancestor worship, 27, 55, 89–90, 107, 142–43, 149
Anesaki Masaharu, 58, 61
Anglican Church, 48, 93, 102–3, 136
Anglo-Japanese Alliance, 54, 60
antireligion movement, 93–94
anti-war activity
  atheists, 94
  Christians, 59, 61
  Hommichi, 100
  Maruyama-kyō, 50
  Non-Church Movement, 103
  Ōmoto-kyō, 75
  nuclear weapons, movement to ban, 133–34, 136, 152
  See also draft evasion; pacifism; peace movement
Association of Shintō Shrines (Jinja Honchō), 119, 130, 132, 135, 156, 158
atheism, 93–94

bakufu, 4, 6, 8–11, 16, 18–20, 22, 33, 35, 114
bakuhan system, 4–6, 7, 13, 17, 19, 27
banshin, 104
bettō, 6, 22, 24, 29
bosatsu, 22, 90
Buddhism, 19–26, 54–58, 91–93, 104–5, 121–30, 160–61
  denominations, 102, 108, 124–28
  education under, 55, 129, 160
  funeral rites, 7, 9, 55, 113
  international activities, 128–30, 134, 144
  lay movements, 12, 84, 105–7, 125–26, 128, 145, 165
  modernization of, 55–58, 91–93
  parishioners, 5–7, 26, 28, 35, 55, 122–23, 149–50, 160
  persecution of (*haibutsu kishaku*), 19–22, 24–32
  postwar period, 120–30, 160–61
  postwar reform, 124–26, 160–61
  priests, 30, 54, 84, 122–23, 125–26
  separation from Shintō, 8, 22, 24–25, 30
  social programs, 129–30
  " State Buddhism," 56
  temple, main and branch, 5, 124–25, 127
  temple affiliation, 5–7, 26, 28, 35, 149, 160
  temple estates, 26, 122–23
  temple reorganization, 124–26
  temples, and tourism, 123
  war effort, cooperation in, 118, 121
  war effort, repent cooperation in, 119
  wedding rites, 58
Buddhist Federation (Bukkyō Rengōkai), 126, 128

179

Buddhist Political Alliance, 130
Buddhist sects and schools
  Hanazonokai, 128
  Hokke (Lotus) sect, 12
  Hossō sect, 124
  Jōdo (Pure Land) sect, 14, 26, 28, 89, 104–5, 122, 124, 127–28, 160
  Jōdo Shinshū Honganji sect, 26, 28, 31, 91, 127–28, 158–59, 160
  Kōyasan Shingon sect, 124
  Kurama Kōkyō, 124
  Kūkai sect, 124
  Myōshinji, 128
  Nakayama Myō sect, 124
  Nichiren sect, 17, 50, 58, 88, 104–5, 107, 122, 124–25, 134, 140, 150, 152
  Nichiren sect, Shōretsu branch, 17, 107–8
  Nichiren Shōshū, 107–8, 148–50, 154, 164–65
    See also Sōka Gakkai
  Rinzai sect, 128
  Shingon sect, 86, 122, 128, 141, 143
  Shinshū Ōtani sect, 56–57, 125, 127, 158–59, 160–61
  Shōkannon sect, 124
  Shōtoku sect, 124
  Shugen sect, 124
  Tendai sect, 106, 124–25, 143, 160
  Wa sect, 124
Buddhist Social Alliance (Bukkyō Shakai Dōmei), 126
Bureau of Educational Affairs, 115
Bureau of Religion, 68, 83, 115
Bureau of Shrines, 68, 101
Bussho Gonenkai, 89, 143, 158, 163, 165

capitalism, 9, 30, 45, 54–55, 60–61, 68, 70, 72–73, 82–83, 85, 92, 121, 131, 137, 146–47, 149, 153, 155, 157
Catholicism, 5, 34–36, 63–65, 103, 137, 161
  churches, 34
  martyrdom, 35
  Mary (Santa Maria), 34, 98
  papal embassy, 103
  Second Vatican Council, 162
  Urakami (hidden) Christians (kakure kirishitan), 34–40, 63
    See also Christianity
Chion-in, 124, 127–28

Christian Federation of Japan (Nihon Kirisuto-kyō Remmei), 93
Christianity, 9, 12, 30–33, 35–38, 46, 55, 58–64, 91–93, 102–3, 121–22, 133, 137, 156, 164
  chaplains, 59, 102
  prohibition of, 5, 10, 22–23, 33, 35, 37–38, 98
  social movements, 59–64, 158–59
  social work, 59–64, 93, 122, 137–38
  war effort, cooperation in, 121, 161
    See also Catholicism; missionary work; Protestantism; under specific denominations
Christian Peace Association, 133, 135
Christian socialism, 61–64, 93
Church of Christ in Japan (Nihon Kirisuto Kyōkai), 37–38, 46, 48, 102
Clark, W. S., 39–40
clergy, 64, 145
    See also Buddhism, priests; Catholicism; Christianity; missionary work; Shintō, shrine priests
Cold War, 133, 137
cold water ablutions, 89–90, 114
colonialism, 111–13
communism. See Marxism
Communist Party, 155, 159, 165
Confucianism, 5–10, 23, 25, 37–38, 46, 48, 88, 91, 113, 144
Constitution, Meiji, 47–48, 58, 65, 101, 110
Constitution, postwar, 120–21, 135, 152, 158–59, 166–67
Council of State, 21, 29
" culture and enlightenment," 28, 30, 33

Dainichi Nyorai, 86–87
Dai Nihon Kannonkai (Greater Japan Kannon Association), 104–5, 140–41
    See also Sekai Kyūsei-kyō
dancing religion (odoru shūkyō). See Tenshō Kōtai Jingū-kyō
democracy, 68, 118–19, 121, 124–26, 128, 133, 137–38, 154, 159, 165, 166–67
Democratic Sociaist Party, 153, 155–56, 165–66
Department of Shintō, 6, 21, 23, 29, 65, 102

divination, 107
Divine Wind. *See kamikaze*
Divine Wind League (Shimpūren),
   39
Dōbōkai Undō (Brotherhood Move-
   ment), 127, 160–61
Dōin (Tao Yuan), 75
Dōshisha English School, 39, 61
draft evasion, and conscientious ob-
   jection, 50, 102
Dutch Reformed Church, 36–37

eeja-naika disturbances, 19–20
emperor
   declaration of humanity, 119, 121,
      139, 158
   divine status of, 20, 73, 75, 77–79,
      110, 119, 132, 139, 158
   enshrined *kami*, 66
   movement to revere, 13, 18, 48
   religious authority of, 18, 20–21,
      43, 47, 139
   sacred regalia of, 3, 29, 99, 110,
      131, 158
emperor system, xvi, 9, 33, 38, 43,
   48, 69, 71, 95–109, 110–11, 114,
   119, 125, 132, 140, 157–60, 163,
   166
emperor worship, 23, 29, 44, 58, 65,
   86, 90, 98, 104–5, 114
Empire Day (Kigensetsu), 132
   See also Kenkoku Kinenbi
Ennō-kyō, 142
equality between sexes, 15, 16
era names (*gengō*) legislation, 158
established religions, xvi, 50, 74, 84–
   85, 91–93, 145–46, 149
   See also under specific religions

family system, 14, 38, 46, 88, 90–91,
   123, 137, 139, 142, 147
farmers' cooperatives, 63
farmers' movements, 93
fascism, 82, 85–86, 88, 92, 96–97,
   101, 118, 139–40
February 26th Incident, 101
feudalism, 4–13, 18, 24, 25, 36, 71–
   72, 91
folk religion, 12, 16, 29, 41, 71, 87,
   131, 143
   See also magic; shamanism
Freedom and Popular Rights Movement, 46–47
freedom of religion, xvi, 31, 43, 96,
   118–136, 145, 147, 156, 159, 162,
   166–67

Friendship Association. *See* Yūaikai
Fuji, Mt., 8, 43, 49, 108, 134
Fujidō sect, 8
Fuji pilgrimage groups, 8, 41, 43, 49
Fukuzawa Yukichi, 47
Fusō-kyō, 43

Gandhi, 134
Gandhi Peace Alliance, 133
Gedatsukai, 144
General Council of Trade Unions of
   Japan, 133
gokoku jinja, 67, 160
government, and Buddhism, unity of
   (*ōbutsu myōgō*), 58, 88, 109, 148,
   152, 154
government, and religion
   separation of, 31, 42–43, 118–36,
      156, 159, 160, 162, 166–67
   unity of, xv, 20, 43, 154, 156
government, recognition of religion,
   8, 43–46, 145
government, suppression of religion,
   10–11, 17, 22–24, 26, 33–36, 50–
   51, 70, 72–75, 78–79, 92–93, 95–
   109 121, 145
Greater East Asia Co-Prosperity
   Sphere, 113, 134
Greater Teaching Academy (Taikyō-
   In), 29, 30, 31, 41

hakkō ichiu, 110–11
harvest festival, 20
healing, 11–14, 16, 31, 49–51, 71–72,
   76, 87–88, 90, 105, 140, 142, 145,
   148
Heiminsha (Society of Common
   People), 61
Higashi Honganji, 127, 161
Hiranuma cabinet, 101
Hiranuma Kiichirō, 109
Hirata Atsutane, 8–10
Hito no Michi Kyōdan, 86–88, 91,
   95, 98–99
   See also Perfect Liberty Kyōdan
Holiness Organization, 93
holy wars, 113, 118
Hommichi, 75–79, 91, 95, 99–100
   Doroumi Kōki, 77, 100
Hommon Butsuryū-kō, 12, 17–18,
   87–88, 134
Hōnen, 127
Honganji, 161
Hōtoku-sha (Society for the Repay-
   ment of Virtue), 91
human rights, 163

Imperial Buddhism (Kōdō Bukkyō), 104
" imperial Christianity " (Kōdō Kirisutokyō), 102
imperialism, 20–22, 73, 75, 92, 110–15, 162
Imperial Rescript on Education, 47, 59, 87, 98, 110
Inari faith, 72, 139
Inari shrines, 20
Ise Shrine, 15, 19, 23, 27, 41–43, 47, 72, 90, 108, 113, 119, 131–32, 158, 163
Ishida Baigan, 7
Ishinkai. *See* Meidōkai
Ishin Remmei, 145
Ittōen, 57
Iwakura Tomomi, 37
Izumo Ōyashiro-kyō, 43
Izumo Taisha, 42, 72

Japan
    Allied Occupation of, 118–32, 137, 141–44, 146–47
    rearmament of, 137
    U.S. military bases in, 134
Japanese Christian Believers Friendship Conference, 46–47
Japanese Conference of World Pacifists, 135
Japanese Religion and Peace Movement, 135
Japanese Religionists Council for Peace (Nihon Shūkyōsha Heiwa Kyōgikai), 166
jichin, 159
Jimmu, Emperor, 20, 67, 110–11
Jindō Tokumitsu-kyō. *See* Hito no Michi Kyōdan
Jingū Hōsaikai, 43, 45
Jinja Honchō. *See* Association of Shintō Shrines
Jiu-kyō, 139
Jizō, 26, 97

Kagawa Toyohiko, 62, 93
Kakushin-kyō. *See* Shintō Tenkōkyo
kami, 7, 9, 11–12, 14–15, 20–23, 27, 30, 41–42, 49, 66–67, 69, 71–76, 84, 87–89, 99, 104, 108–14, 121, 131–32, 138–39, 140
    divine (*akitsu mi kami*), 110
    land of the (Shinkoku Nippon), 114–15, 121
    living (*ikigami*), 10–13, 16, 49–50, 77, 79, 84, 110, 138, 140

    manifest (*arahito-gami*), 23, 47, 77–79, 110, 114
    parent (*oyagami*), 14, 77
    possession by, 11, 14, 71, 74, 76, 89, 90, 106, 139
kamikaze (divine wind), 115
Kannagi-be Shintō. *See* Shinri-kyō
Kannon, 26, 97, 105
Kawade Bunjirō. *See* Konkō-kyō, Konkō Daijin
Kenkoku Kinenbi (National Foundation Day), 132, 158
Ketsumeidan (Blood Brotherhood), 92
Kiitsu Kyōkai (Unity Church), 61
Kingdom of God Movement (Kami no Kuni Undō), 93
Kinoshita Naoe, 61
Kiyozawa Manshi, 56, 160–61
kō, 14
Kōdō Chi-kyō, 145
Kōdō-ha, 96
Kōdō Kyōdan, 106, 144
Kojiki, 9
Kokuchūkai, 58, 69, 88, 92, 106, 132
kokutai (national polity), 86
Konjin, 15–16, 71, 107
Konkō-kyō, 12, 15–17, 31, 44–46, 49, 71, 100, 134, 138
Konkō Daijin, 15–16, 45
Korea, 112–13, 153–54, 163–64
Korean War, 133, 137, 146, 148
kōsha, 17, 144
Kōtoku Shūsui, 61
Kōya, Mt., 86
Kumamoto Band, 39
Kurozumi-kyō, 12–13, 41, 45
Kwangtung Army, 112

labor problems, 55, 60, 82, 93
labor unions, 62–64, 133, 153
lèse majesté, 44, 47, 70, 73, 74–75, 78, 95, 97–100, 103, 108, 139
Liberal Democratic Party, 132, 153, 155, 159, 165–66
living Buddha (*ikibotoke*), 143
Lotus Sutra, 17, 50–51, 57–58, 88–92, 104, 106–9, 134, 142–43, 147–48

magic, 13, 20, 22, 31, 51, 84–85, 87–90, 98, 105, 107–8, 138, 143–45, 149
    See also folk religion
Maruyama-kyō, 44, 49–50, 70, 134–35

Marxism, 91–93, 130, 133, 135–36
Medical Practioners Law, 105
Meidōkai, 85
Meiji Centennial celebration, 157
Meiji, Emperor, 42, 57, 60, 69, 112–13
Meiji Shrine (Jingū), 69–70
Meiji Six Society (Meirokusha), 30
Methodist Church, 40, 48
Miki Takeo, 159
militarism, 64–65, 68, 82–115, 118–19
  postwar revival of, 132–33, 159, 162
Ministry of Army and Navy, 113
Ministry of Civil Affairs, 28
Ministry of Education, 65, 68, 83, 85, 115
Ministry of Home Affairs, 66, 68, 78, 83, 96–97, 100, 113
Ministry of Religious Education, 29, 31, 37, 41
Miroku Bosatsu, 49, 71, 74, 85, 97, 163
Misogi-kyō, 43
missionary work, 7, 14, 17, 36–37, 45–50, 57, 72–73, 83–84, 105–6, 118, 137, 146
Mitake-kyō. See Ontake-kyō
Moralogy (Dōtoku Kagaku), 91
Motoori Norinaga, 8
mountain ascetics (yamabushi), 14, 18, 46, 87
mountain pilgrimage groups, 12, 31–32, 41, 46, 49
Mugaen, 57
Myōchikai, 143–44, 158, 165
  See also Reiyūkai
Myōdōkai, 143–44

Nakayamashingo-shōshū, 144
National Foundation Day. See Kenkoku Kinenbi
nationalism, 145
  See also patriotism; ultranationalism
Nempōshin-kyō, 144
New Buddhism Friends Association, 56
Newly Arisen Buddhist Youth Alliance, 92–93, 126
new religions, 10–18, 32, 44–46, 48–51, 70–79, 82–91, 95, 125, 127–29, 133, 137–56, 162–65
  See also under specific religions
Nichiren, 17, 58, 107, 149, 154
Nihon Keishin Sūso Jishūdan, 89

Nihon o Mamorukai, 165
Nihon Shoki, 9
Nihonzan Myōhōji, 88, 104, 134–35
Niijima Jō, 38–39
Ninigi-no-Mikoto, 99, 110
Ninomiya Sontoku, 57
Nishi Honganji, 28, 54, 56–57, 127
Nitobe Inazō, 40
Nomonhan Incident, 112
Non-Church Movement, 61, 103
norito, 9
Nosaka Sanzō, 63
Nyorai-kyō, 12, 104

Occupation. See Japan, Allied Occupation of
ōkage mairi, 15, 19
Ōkuma Shigenobu, 35
Ōkuninushi, 9, 21, 42
Ommyōdō. See Taoism
Ōmoto-kyō, 70–75, 85–86, 88, 91, 95–99, 104, 133–35, 140, 166
  Asano Wasaburō, 73–74, 139
  Deguchi Nao, 70–72, 74
  Deguchi Onisaburō, 72–74, 78, 95–98, 138
  First Ōmoto Incident, 74–75, 78, 85
  fumie, 98
  Ofudesaki, 71, 73
onomancy, 107, 143
Ontake, Mt., 41, 43, 73, 86–87
Ontake-kyō, 73, 86–87
Orthodox Church, 137
Orthodox Church of America, 138
Ōtani Kōchō, Abbot, 160–61

pacifism, 49, 72–73, 98, 100, 133
  See also anti-war activities; peace movement
patriotism, 31, 38–39, 48, 54, 58, 65, 74, 90
peace movement, 132–136, 158–59
  See also anti-war activities; pacifism
Perfect Liberty (PL) Kyōdan, 141–42, 144, 158–59, 162, 165
  See also Hito no Michi Kyōdan
postwar society, 144–47
Potsdam Declaration, 118
Presbyterian Church in Japan, 38, 46
prostitution, 60
Protestantism, 35–40, 46–48, 55, 92–93, 133, 137, 138
revival, 47
  See also under specific denominations

Public Peace and Order Police Law, 65
Public Peace Preservation Law, 78, 82, 95, 97, 99, 103, 108

reactionary politics, 157, 165–67
Reiyūkai, 88–91, 105–6, 142–43, 163, 165
　Kotani Kimi, 89, 105–6, 142–43, 163
　Kubo Kakutarō, 88–90, 105
　Niwano Nikkyō, 106, 143, 162
religion, and politics, 65, 151–56, 163, 164–67
religion, statistics, xvi, 6, 10, 13, 27, 46–47, 50, 57, 63, 66, 83, 85–87, 98, 102, 107–8, 112, 122, 127, 130–31, 142, 145, 148, 154, 168–71
religions, traditional, 5–10
　See also under specific religions
religious cooperation, 61, 64, 75, 132–36, 162
Religious Corporations Ordinance (Shūkyō Hōjin Rei), 119, 124, 145
Religious Juridical Persons Law, 145
Religious Organizations Law (Shū-kyō Dantai Hō), 95, 101–2, 107, 109, 114, 119, 124, 131
Remmon-kyō, 44, 50–51, 70, 88
right-wing patriotic movements, 82, 96, 132, 158
right-wing religious movements, 140
riots, 5, 39, 68, 82
Risshō Kōseikai, 106–7, 135, 143–44, 147, 153, 158–59, 162–63, 165
　Naganuma Myōkō, 106, 143
ritual, and government, unity of, 20–21, 22, 23, 29, 41, 43
Russian Orthodox Church (Harisu-tosu), 64, 102–3, 137
Russo-Japanese War, 54–55, 57, 59, 60–61, 64–65, 113

salvation, 83–85, 90, 146–47
Salvation Army, 59–61, 93, 103
San Francisco Peace Treaty, 132, 144, 147–48
sangaku shinkō, 144
Sect Shintō-Buddhist-Christian Religious Assembly, 68
Seichō no Ie, 73, 85–86, 91, 104, 132, 140, 142, 158, 163, 165–66
　" bright thought " (kōmyō shisō), 86
　Political Alliance, 163
Seigikai Kyōdan, 143

Sekai Kyūsei-kyō, 140–42, 144, 163, 165
Sekai Meshiya-kyō (World Messiah Religion). See Sekai Kyūsei-kyō
semi-religious organizations, 83
separation of state and religion. See government, and Buddhism, unity of; government, and religion, sepa-ration of; government, and religion, unity of; ritual, and government, unity of
shamanism, 72, 84, 89–90, 105, 138, 143, 145
shasō, 6, 22
Shingaku, 7, 12
Shinnyo-en, 144
Shinran, 127, 161
Shinri-kyō, 43
Shinshū-kyō, 43
Shintō, 6–10, 20–24, 27–33, 41–44, 65–69, 110–17, 130–36, 158–60
　doctrine, 19, 42–43, 71, 131, 144
　funeral rites, 6–7, 9, 22, 43, 113
　nonreligious function of, 42–43, 132
　parishioners, 28, 66, 131
　postwar revivalist movement, 130–32
　Restoration, 8–11, 21, 27–28, 41, 111
　Sect, 41–46, 65, 84, 91, 99, 102, 121, 138
　separation from Buddhism, 22, 24–25, 30
　Shrine, xv–xvi, 6, 65, 84, 119, 130, 132, 137, 149, 153, 159–60
　State, xv–xvi, 22, 28, 41–46, 50–51, 63, 65, 66–68, 70, 84, 101, 110–11, 114, 119, 121, 131–32, 138, 147, 156, 158–60, 163, 166
　shrine estates, 26–27, 97, 113, 130
　shrine priests, 27, 42, 47, 66, 130
　shrine ranks, 27, 43, 66–67, 111–12
　shrines, 27, 42–43, 54, 66–69, 111, 119, 121, 130–32
　shrines, overseas, 111–13
　war effort, cooperation in, 121
　wedding rites, 58
Shintō-Buddhist amalgamation, 30–31
Shintō Honkyoku, 43
Shintō Ministry, 29, 102
Shintō Office, 21, 31–32, 41–43
Shintō schools
　Hirata, 10, 22, 25, 36

Kokugaku, 8–10, 22–23, 25
Mito, 10
Shirakawa, 6, 8, 16, 21–22
Suika, 6
Watarai, 6
Yoshida, 6, 14, 21–22
Yoshikawa, 6
Shintō Section, Council of State, 21
Shintō Shūsei sect, 41
Shintō Tenkōkyo, 85
Shishinkai, 106
Shizensha (Nature Society), 87
shōbō, 17, 108, 150
Shōkannon sect, 124
shōkonsha, 67, 113–14
Shōtoku sect, 124
Shrine Board, 102
Shugendō, 90
    See also mountain ascetics
Shūkyō Seiji Kenkyū Kai, 166
Shūyō-dan (Improvement Organi-
    zation), 91
Sino-Japanese War (1894–95), 50,
    54, 60, 65, 80, 111
Sino-Japanese War (1937–45), 99–
    101, 110–13
Social-Christian Alliance, 93
social classes, 4, 8–9, 11, 13, 16, 42,
    45, 47, 76, 83, 90, 99, 108, 122,
    141, 146–47, 149, 151, 154
Social Democratic Party, 61
socialism, 57
    Buddhism, 92
    Christian, 61–64
    Japan Socialist Party, 155
    Kōmeitō, 165
    Sōka Gakkai, 153
    Unification Church, 164
social problems, 55–56, 62, 73, 75,
    82–83, 91, 93, 144, 146, 149
Society for the Study of Socialism, 61
Sōdōmei (General Alliance), 63
Sōka Gakkai, 107–9, 130, 135, 147–
    56, 164–66
    aggressive proselytism (shakubuku),
        108, 148, 150–51, 155
    cemeteries, litigation over burial
        in, 150–51
    Daigohonzon, 108, 149
    Ikeda Daisaku, 148, 152, 154–55,
        164
    Kokuritsu Kaidan, 148, 151, 164
    Kōmeitō, 154–56, 164–65, 166
    kōsen rufu, 148, 165
    Makiguchi Tsunesaburō, 107, 109
    Shōhondō, 164–65

Taisekiji, 148, 151, 164
Toda Jōsei, 107, 109, 148
Sonnō Hōbutsu Daidōdan (Revere the
    Emperor and Serve the Buddha
    Federation), 48
Sorge spy incident, 103
Southern Court, 67, 139
Student Christian Movement, 93
sun, 12–13, 87–88, 98–99
Sun Goddess. See Amaterasu Ōmi-
    kami

Taigyaku Incident, 57, 62, 64
Taisei-kyō, 43, 50
Taisha-kyō, 43
Taishō Democracy, 68
Taishō, Emperor, 58, 74
Taishō Restoration. 74
Taoism, religious, 16, 144
Tenchi Kōdō Zenrinkai. See Zen-
    rinkai
Tenri-kyō, 13–15, 31, 44–45, 48–49,
    68, 70–72, 75–76, 85–86, 100–101,
    106, 134, 138
    Doroumi Kōki, 15, 44, 72, 100
    Iburi Izō, 48, 76
    jiba, 15, 77
    Nakayama Miki, 14–15, 44–45, 48,
        70, 76–77
    Ofudesaki, 44
Tenri-Ō-no-Mikoto, 14–15, 44, 70, 76
Tenshin-kyō, 145
Tenshō Kōtai Jingū-kyō, 139–40
this-worldly benefits, 10–11, 16–17,
    27, 42, 48–50, 84, 88, 90, 100, 108,
    123, 130, 138, 142, 144–45, 148–50
thought control, 78, 93, 94–95, 104
Tohokami Shintō, 8, 43
Tokumitsu-kyō, 86, 91
Tokumitsu-kyōkai, 87
Tokutomi Roka, 39, 62
Tokutomi Sohō, 39
Tōyama Mitsuru, 96

Uchida Ryōhei, 96
Uchimura Kanzō, 40, 47, 59, 61, 93
ujigami, 16
ultranationalism, 48, 87, 119
Unification Church (Genri Kenkyū-
    kai, Sekai Kirisuto Tōitsu Shinrei
    Kyōkai), 163–64
Union of New Religious Organiza-
    tions of Japan (Shin Nihon Shū-
    kyō Dantai Rengōkai), 135, 147,
    156, 162–63, 165
Unitarianism, 61

United Church of Christ in Japan (Nihon Kirisuto Kyōkai), 46, 48, 138, 161–62
Unity Christianity Liberal Association, 62
universal suffrage, 68, 82
Urakami Christians. See Catholicism, Urakami Christians
urbanization, 55, 83, 130, 146–47
U.S.-Japan Security Treaty, 130–31, 132, 135, 152, 156, 165
Uten sect, 8

Vietnam War, 166

World Conference on Religion and Peace (Sekai Shūkyōsha Heiwa Kaigi), 162
Japanese Committee, 163
World Federation of Religions for the Promotion of Peace Conference (Sekai Rempō Heiwa Sokushin Shūkyōsha Taikai), 166

World Religionists' Peace Conference, 135
world renewal, 12, 15, 19, 50, 70–79, 85, 139, 149
World War I, 68, 73, 75–76, 83, 97, 113
World War II, xv, 86, 86, 101–3, 108–9, 110–15, 159

Xavier, St. Francis, 5

yamabushi. See mountain ascetics
Yanagita Kunio, 66
Yanaihara Tadao, 103
Yasukuni Shrine, 21, 67, 113–14, 132, 158–60, 162–63, 166
Bill, 158–59
YMCA, 47, 93
Yūaikai (Friendship Association), 62–64

Zen boom, 129
Zenrinkai, 142